THE LOCKDOWN ON SELF-LOVE

How to make suffering work for you

ANTONIO DE SOUSA

First published in United Kingdom 2022

Editor, Annie Percik

This book is part-memoir. It reflects the author's, and only the author's, present recollections of experiences over time. Some names and characteristics have been changed, some events have been compressed, and some dialogue has been recreated.

ISBN: 9798432843821

TABLE OF CONTENTS

I would like to dedicate this book to the man I once was.

I thank you for the troubles, challenges and tribulations.

I know it's not been easy but, without you, there would be no present I.

FOREWORD BY ALI CHAMBERS

I remember the first time Antonio and I met over Facebook Messenger. He had left his parents' house and driven to a secluded spot, so we could have our meeting in private. It was here that I recognsied the first of Antonio's challenges; the lack of support in his life.

We discussed his book, why he hadn't been able to get past the first chapter (a common issue with debut authors), and then I set him my favourite exercise. I asked him to write out a timeline of his life and just to witness which memories came up. You'll see them throughout this book. Some were heartbreaking, some were funny, others I felt deep compassion for. It's an emotional experience, and we had to stop a couple of times for Antonio to regain some of his equilibrium. But that timeline formed the basis of the story you are about to read.

Now, with a plan in hand, Antonio dived forward with gusto.

Given some of his experiences, some of the comments people close to him expressed, his dyslexia...Antonio had a myriad of excuses to fall back on, should he have chosen to. He didn't. In the face of adversity, he kept going.

It's the mark of a true writer; resilience. You write until your hands are raw to the bone, your emotions spent, and everyone around you just doesn't get it. Why put yourself through all that suffering? What if it amounts to nothing?

And Antonio had suffered. Sometimes through his own mindset, sometimes it was shown to him through the eyes of others. And here he was, willing to relive it all, if it brought you, the reader, some insights into your own life. Some 'aha' moments, some wisdom, some guidance, as you discover your own path, particularly if you've battled with low self-esteem, emotional insecurities, or addictions of any kind.

What I didn't warn Antonio about was how writing a book would bring it all back up again. You see, the first time, you are living the experiences to learn the lesson. Should you choose to write about them, however, the Universe invites the lessons back into your life, to see if you can handle them from a new perspective, an elevated state. Like taking a step up on the staircase of Spiral Dynamics and facing the same challenge from a new angle. (I'll leave Antonio to talk you through his interpretation of Spiral Dynamics later.)

And so, the challenges came back up. Now, with the personal story in black and white on the paper, a terrifying thing in itself to confront, Antonio was asked to look at the lessons within each memory and share them with you. It took the book to a whole new level and created a conscious framework for how to work through feelings of inadequacy that I don't think Antonio was aware he had been working on this whole time. I could see it, between the lines, but the moment Antonio realised it was a beautiful experience to witness.

It's changed the man he's become. The man I met back in December 2020 was aware but still reactive, practising self-love but not embodying it. As each new challenge has arisen, from lack of support from loved ones to sharing the book with beta readers, to editing and marketing, Antonio has shown up. And each time, he has become better at responding not reacting, analysing not accusing, and taking responsibility, rather than making excuses.

There have been relapses, naturally. That's part of being human. There have been months where he's wanted to quit (and I've ignored him). There have been months in this sixteen-month journey that have been harder than others. And still, Antonio continues to practice the steps he presents to you in this book. He continues up the staircase of his own Spiral Dynamics.

It's been a beautiful metamorphosis to watch, and a privileged journey to be his mentor on, as he wrote his experiences down on paper. I hope you find the insights hidden in these pages as enlightening, supportive, and sometimes challenging, as they were intended to be.

THE LEGEND OF THE DARK KING

There was a legend by the name of The Dark King. His eyes were as black as night and his soul was plagued by chaos, for his shadows would never leave him. Gazing across his kingdom, he saw the land was drenched in darkness and, every day and night, he was tormented by his inner voice of despair, which said the shadows would never leave.

To quiet the voice, the king waged war and conquered lands, hoping desperately to chase the shadows & torment away. One day, when there was nothing left to conquer, standing at the edge of the earth, the sun shining down on his back, the king saw his shadow once more. He began to question if the shadow was his or if it was the voice of despair in his head. He had spent so long running from it, he couldn't quite tell.

But with the sun kissing his back, he remembered how he once used to feel. He felt as if the warmth from the sun was what he himself used to radiate. Slowly, the light of the sun began to envelop him and the voice slowly quietened. A tear ran down his cheek, as he realised the voice in his head was a cry for help, to remember who he truly was.

He was not The Dark King, but A Knight of the Light.

That was who he was born to be.

But, as his mind had become troubled with the thoughts of others, he had dimmed his light and become afraid of the shadows. It was this that had enraged him the most, as he lost his way. The despair that the shadows had brought was not because his soul was in chaos, but because he had forgotten that shadows were supposed to dance in the light.

Can you connect with The Dark King's inner turmoil?

Funny how who we are born to be versus how we are shaped by our life experiences are often two different people. If I have learnt anything, it is that, when these two are not in alignment, you will enter a victim frame of mind, a rather beige stage in your life. Your job is to awaken, to stop chasing the illusion in front of you, and to answer the call of who you really are.

With that in mind, I hope my journey of life experiences I'm about to share not only makes for a good read, but also that, through my lessons, I can help another human being figure out who they are, too.

INTRODUCTION

It is fair to say that certain events led me to write this book. In part, it was my obsession with trying to understand the workings of my own mind and my emotions. But it was also my desire to open up, rather than do the easier thing, which would be to make like the ostrich and bury my head in the sand, like so many of us do.

Not long before I started writing this book, I went through a pretty traumatic experience, which resulted in me losing everything. I saw my world crumbling around me, and I came to realise that I was living with a victim mentality. At the height of it all, I felt miserable, I pitied myself and was constantly depressed. I projected that onto all who loved me, feeling like I wasn't good enough and that everyone was against me. I had no friends of my own and had very little understanding of how to move forward. I lived in a vicious circle that I blamed on circumstances.

I was an emotional mess, and I was angry at the world. I felt like there was no compromise with anything in life and I could see no light at the end of the tunnel. I felt as if my cards had been dealt and this was my fate. But I hadn't addressed my own behaviour up until that point, including my coping mechanisms for how I dealt with my anxiety, for example, or how I conducted myself in confrontational situations.

I didn't take responsibility for my sex addiction or using Class A drugs, either, which I regularly indulged in, using the excuse that I had nothing better to do. In fact, it was something I unfortunately looked forward to, all too much. These behaviours were my coping mechanisms and all they did was mask the pain that I was living with for many years, hide my depression, and mean I had nothing else to look forward to. At least, that is what I led myself to believe.

Recently, I went through a breakup. We have a child together and, as you might imagine, I was going through a rough patch, with a lot of emotions to deal with. One afternoon, after spending most of my time in the lounge with my head buried between my legs, crying, I had this realisation; with every breath in my lungs, I had to get to the bottom of this. I recognised that the relationship I had with myself was fragile and that I needed to work on it. I spoke to myself, perhaps for the first time, and made up my mind, right then and there, to improve. I asked myself how I could make that happen.

I found myself down the path of self-development and personal growth and, from that day on, my life started to improve, as did the relationships I had with others. Most importantly, my relationship with life took a turn for the better. It was as if I was reborn. By that, what I mean to say is, I looked at my own hands for the first time and felt the awe of what it meant to be alive.

One thing led to another, and I ended up having a few experiences that showed me who I truly was — an infinite being, having a human experience. And with that, I found spirituality.

I smoked DMT, which I will go into later, and that helped me shape my perception of my life. I began to understand that, while things might be out of my control, I could at least manage myself better, take it easy, and for the best part, not be so hard on myself. I learnt how to get a handle on my anxiety, and I came to believe in something far greater than myself. It gave me a great deal of strength to know that I wasn't alone and that I was divinely supported. There were still many days when I would feel disheartened, wondering when all the suffering would end. It took a great deal of effort to recommit every day to bettering myself, choosing to believe that I had a choice, that the responsibility was all mine. That I could be a better version of me today than who I had been the day before. And eventually, little by little, my ambition grew and now, here I stand.

Admittedly, choosing to write is also my own way of

making peace with what once consumed me. The lockdown in 2020 caused me to do a lot of reflecting. I wondered to myself, for the first time, what is it that I have to contribute to the world? What is it that I have to offer? I knew many men in my situation had taken their own lives, after splitting up with their baby mamas. So many others also suffered in one way or another, where they also felt like they saw no other way out.

I used to feel so much shame. I felt like I was only existing. I could relate to those who had chosen to take their own lives. The day I lost everything, when my world crumbled around me, the easiest thing I could have done would have been to take my own life. I felt uncomfortable in my own skin and had a hyperactive insecurity, feeling as if everyone knew about my dark secrets.

This fired up a calling within me. I wanted to allow my vulnerability and transparency to set the tone for the truth. The unapologetic truth. We do what we do, for we know no better at the time.

It is also my wish that I inspire another fellow human being and raise awareness about the unhealthiest coping mechanism that I personally lived with: not addressing the elephant in the room. Having the courage & willingness to open up, without sugar-coating anything, to express, to discuss without arguing, and to hold space for one another, is the biggest lesson I have learnt from this journey.

In all honesty, now I think of the word 'argument' and wonder, what is even the point? If I had one wish, I would request that humanity had an interest in having a healthy debate. From there, we would all find middle ground and compromise — I see so much value in that. In love, in full support, in an open mind and heart.

So, to start you on this journey, I would ask you the same question I asked myself at that time in my life. What is life all about, if not for the experience? I mean, look at chocolate ice cream, for example, or your favourite flavour of choice. If it wasn't for the ability, the pleasure, the feeling of how it stimulates your taste buds, if not for that, what would even be the point of it?

I believe our lives are about growth and the evolution of our soul through experience with all the contrasts of life; we wouldn't otherwise have any need to navigate it. If life were plain sailing, we would all be lost at sea. Having said that, I firmly believe that those who do find themselves lost, as I once did myself for many years, have simply lost the spark within themselves.

Perhaps, like me, they might be ungrateful and have a victim mentality. I remember once being called ignorant about this and I took that to heart. I felt as though my intelligence was being questioned and found it patronising, to say the least. But here is what I learnt. Ignorance is the expression to say that one does not know. My ignorance was my lack of understanding as to what the term "victim" meant and what it meant to live with a victim frame of mind. Before I understood it, I would most likely have taken offence at being called a victim and gone on the defensive, unaware that my very reaction proved the point. I was oblivious to the fact that I had fallen victim to the circumstances happening to me and took very little control over how I chose to engage. Instead, I chose to react.

Once I understood the victim mindset, though, I was able to respond rather than react to life. If someone said that to me now, I'd be more inclined to say, "You have an interesting point of view, I would love for you to share your thoughts with me. I would like to understand." Don't make allowances for letting life happen to you, rather than being the reason that life happens.

I also recall being called selfish far too many times in the past. I used to find guilt in that. For my selfishness, I was made to feel shame. I wonder how many of us point the finger to say to another, "All you care about is yourself!" Looking back now, how ridiculous that statement sounds. I didn't care about myself at all at the time. I came to learn that the hard way and at a great cost to me, for many years suffering from depression. When the reality of the fact was obvious; of course I deserved to care about myself!

It's a different attitude, the attitude of "where ain't love if not from within." If you come to think of it, your ability to feel any emotion in the first place comes from inside of you. We're led to believe that it's the responsibility of whatever is outside of you that triggers that response, but that is far from the truth. You get to choose how you feel instead and I imagine (all too well, as I feel the same) that we all want to be happy and feel loved. So, why not offer that to yourself? The responsibility towards oneself is to offer your own self support, to be your own best friend, to be your own cheerleader. To be the one you can count on, no matter what. Have your own back! From there, not only do you benefit by showing up for yourself, but the rest of the world does also, when the best of you gives back what you've got to give to the world. If only we all had this attitude, how much better this world would be!

In my quest to understand, control and make peace with myself and all the choices I have made thus far, I wrote this book. And what I have come to learn is that all experiences, however you label them, are worth sharing. For that's what it's all about: the abundance of contrast. After all, that's what makes up life.

Before we continue into my world and my discovery of

self-love, I would like you to consider this exercise and imagine what the experience would be like for you, if another version of yourself materialised before your own eyes and asked you these questions. How is it that I can love you better? How can I make you feel more supported? How is it that I can be of service to you? What areas in our life would you like to improve on and is there anything that I can do to help?

For me, I heavily depended on all of this from others. Never had it crossed my mind that I should have been offering it to myself all this time.

CHAPTER ONE:
HIDING THE INNER CHILD

It's hard to recall the distant memory of our beginning, the lease of life into this world as a newborn. I ponder on the idea of whether our first cry in the world is our first "traumatic" experience. As if what the mother must endure isn't bad enough, I can only imagine the discomfort of the process of being forced out.

As a baby, imagine experiencing sight and all the other senses for the first time. I have no doubt that this moment is one of awe, not just for the parents, but also for the newborn, who is challenged in understanding the world and life itself, between one push and the next. Can you imagine what it must have been like, seeing life outside of the familiar comfort of the womb for the first time? This is not an easy question to answer, but it's one which, if you dive deep within, can give you a sense of awareness from then to now, at how far you've come and how you have evolved into the person you are today.

A newborn is, or should be, cared for and shown unconditional love. This is the start of his/her development in the world and an internal recognition that they are the most significant person in their own life.

I recall back to when I first witnessed my firstborn crawl, his determination stemming from inspiration. He was eager to approach me, with me having spent hours cuddled up to him. I laid him on the floor, surrounded by toys, so I could attend to the washing up, and there he was, coming at me with wide eyes and the most magnificent smile, full of pride and excitement at his progress. I will never forget that moment.

When I think about "our" first attempt at walking, I am reminded of babies. What if, like babies, we resisted the thought to say to ourselves, 'I can't do it, there is no point anymore. I keep falling either way, perhaps I'm not meant to walk.' Or, 'I'm good as I am, there is no need for me to walk as I am comfortable, my parents will aid me with whatever I need, either way.' In this manner, progress would never occur.

We get up and fall, yet we get up again and we follow this process, until we take one step forward. Then another and another. Then, before you know it, you're riding a bike! This reminds me of the teachings from the Tao; a journey of a thousand miles begins with the first step. And so it is, that the journey to mastery and freedom in any area of our lives begins also with just one step.

Curiosity is the essence of human existence. We are

eager to learn and explore, especially that which elevates excitement and interest. In all of us *that* is what makes us different. What has our attention is where we place focus in life, even when we are but babies.

We start to talk as toddlers, and it is then that the true adventure begins to unfold. Fortunately, or unfortunately, we become a by-product of our environment around us, including the interest, influence, as well as the emotional and mental support of those with whom we grow up.

I grew up in what most would call a normal household, but my parents were conditioned by their past (as are we all) and so I soaked up their conditioning also. There is nothing wrong with that, of course, as it made me who I am today. Everyone's upbringing shapes who they are. The decisions we make, mistakes and choices, the satisfaction & joy or dissatisfaction and distress we feel, are the reality of that which is experience.

But these experiences can shape us so much more than we understand at the time, especially as children. I know this now, by carefully examining my own memories.

I was born in South Africa and my parents had a maid, who looked after me while they were at work. She would drop me off at school and watch me when I got back.

However, when I was home alone, she would lock me in the house. I imagine now it was to keep me safe, while she went about and ran her errands. At four to five years old, I wasn't any the wiser. All I noticed was that I was alone and all the doors were locked. I would bang on the door, but no one would come. I would get up on the kitchen counter, look out the window and cry out for help and attention, which made me feel like I wasn't seen or heard at all.

Who would have thought that this is where it all began for me? My insecurities blossomed from the lack of security I felt at such a young age, when I did not feel safe in my own home on my own, scared and helpless, needing attention. I came from a loving environment indeed, but the consequences of certain events – even with the best of intentions for me at the time – had undesirable effects, growing up.

Along the way, in my childhood, my subconscious took note of whenever I was told that my actions were bad, or the way I expressed myself was wrong, until I believed that it was so. It's a consequence that, until I began my healing journey, caused me not to trust myself or my own reactions to events and/or people.

In another childhood memory, my parents had made me a sandwich and I had decided not to finish it and, instead, hide it behind the cupboard. Only the child in me at the time knows why, but it's something many of us have done. Once my parents found it, mouldy and stinking up the place, I got a few smacks on the bum. Now, I wonder if it was ok for me to be hidden away but not the food. Was I depreciated more than food? Was food more important than me? Is that what the child in me was subconsciously picking up?

These memories demonstrate to me the emotional and mental pain, conflict, and growth that the inner child in me felt. My point being, the memories I clearly retained as a child had a significant impact on the man I became. It is clear the emotions embedded in these memories are raw enough to still create vivid experiences in my mind. From mental and emotional pain to physical pain, I learnt in those formative years (as all of us did) that pain has a profound impact on your life. And because it was never addressed at the time, it had a negative consequence, one way or another. For trauma carries on throughout the rest of our lives, until we heal it...as I will demonstrate in this book.

It is with regret that mindfulness is not a key subject from day one for our children. Poor mental health is a development from the times that we were made unhappy; our loss and dissatisfaction often stem from trauma. For example, as a child, I might have been yelled at for being silly. For me, I was enjoying myself, but for whatever reason, it may have come across as me being “naughty” or not "normal" by their standards and so they yelled at me. From there, I might, perhaps, start to distrust the dialogue and humour I have with my own self and start to believe it to be "bad." This is the early stages of ambivalence and poor self-talk.

Would you agree that children are not always taught how to deal with their emotions or how to process whatever situation they're going through effectively? For example, throwing soft toys is an excellent way to express anger, yet instead, we often raise our voices at children doing this, seeing them as stepping out of line. What they then typically do is follow our lead on how to behave. They mimic our behaviour.

Don't get me wrong; I have yelled at my kids. It's something I'm not proud of, I must admit. I am so thankful I have now learned to comfort my children and affirm to myself that my words are soft, gentle, and loving. As best as I can, in whichever situation I find myself in with my children, I strive to not get aggravated, no matter how many times I have to repeat myself to them. I make them aware of their choices and, if they would like to do things differently, I explore those options with them.

It is my hope that they feel safe and trust that I want what's best for them and give them their own freedom to express who they are. That is how I am choosing to teach them about intentions & the responsibility they have over their own actions.

Within us all lies a complexity of the mind and inner chemistry on how to manage our responses. What I have learnt is that our beliefs are formed by neural connections and that, the bigger the emotion, be it pleasure or pain, the stronger the connection that is formed. An emotion in the mind is connected to an experience perceived and thus you have your belief. And conformity of our responses is a development from the appraisal of doing "right" and the disapproval of whatever may be going "wrong."

The responsibility lies with coming to understand *how* the thought you are having is serving you & if the emotion you're experiencing does also. Because your body ties the emotion & thought back to that original belief. Remember that example I gave you earlier on: being yelled at for being silly? What would come up for me whenever someone had a go at me from then on would be that original feeling that I was wrong for being who I was. This response became amplified and cemented over time. I'll be honest, now and again it made me pretty temperamental and quick to react, which it turns out is perfectly normal, because that's the mode your body takes when it feels threatened. It always goes back to that first experience. It makes the term "you're too emotionally involved" a bit redundant, when you think about it.

This wasn't just helpful for me to understand, but it also gave me insight about my children and everyone else's reactions, too. To not be quick to find fault or pass blame, but understand the paradigm of how their brain works.

I'll leave you with what I have recently discovered about the latest in neuroscience. It is suggested that we only begin to self-regulate our responses at eleven years of age (and that is if we grow up in a healthy environment). We cannot actually consciously change our nervous system responses, until we are at least twenty-five years of age. Interesting, right? Until then, our systems are still reacting and cementing responses. This research has only come through in the last ten years, so we can see how important it is to understand how our brains process experiences, for the sake of our children's future behaviour and happiness in life.

If you're interested in more, I encourage you to look up the paper 'Maturation of the adolescent brain,' published in 2013 by Arain et al, with Dove Medical Press Ltd.

Imagine if, at school, we weren't only taught how to solve solutions and challenges such as mathematics and science, but about our evolution and inner workings, too. To think that our own thoughts are nothing but a matter of neural processes, which consist of past experiences that are attached by emotions, and our everyday circumstances are a combination of connections. How fascinating to come to understand that our emotions and brain activity are, in short, a chemical reaction.

Now, I'm no scientist but let me share with you my own insights on the research I found that fascinated me.

The architecture of the brain is a living organism, made up of mechanics that are all engineered to work together. These consist of three main components: the forebrain, the midbrain and the hindhead. The complexity involved in communication by sending signals throughout the brain, down the spinal cord and then throughout the system is its own study. But something more complex emerges: human consciousness. It emerges on the interface between three components of behaviour; communication, play & the use of tools, so that we may engage with our world. I believe these tools are essential to our inner child, who holds the curious mind.

I'll express our consciousness in two separate parts: the superconscious and the subconscious.

The superconscious I see as our higher faculties. With attention, we can work on evolving our higher faculties, so we can be of our highest good, in connection with Source flowing through us, God, or the Universe. Essentially, it is the best version of you in a super state of awareness, of not only yourself, but in presence with the essence of "your highest expectation of yourself, your highest self and the 'I am' in the present moment of awareness."

What are your higher faculties, might I add? Your faculties are your perception, your will, your imagination, your memory, your reason, and your intention. These can all be developed with intention & perseverance, at any age.

The subconscious is where it gets interesting. There is a saying in the metaphysical science community, "it's as if the universe played a joke on us." Because everything we come to understand, even now as adults, is all that we have soaked up from childhood; every belief, how you see the world, your values, your attitude, how you see yourself and how you conduct yourself, is a simple programming of all the nurturing and conditioning to date. Take the food you like, as an example. Somewhere along the line, if you look deep enough, you will come to learn that not only your mother and father might have enjoyed the same food that you do, but that someone far down your ancestral line liked it, and so it was passed on. There is so much wisdom in this field of consciousness. It's one that we take for granted, unaware of our power and capabilities, because we're not aware of our conditioning and that we can, with effort, re-condition ourselves.

If you think about it, who you think you are ain't you at

all, but a by-product of your environment & lots of people!

It's unfortunate, really, that growing up, we come to believe that we must abandon the child within us. We tell our children to stop acting so childishly, when are they going to grow up, they're so immature...etc. Sure, there are responsibilities to be met & this sense of having to conform into an identity which is professional and responsible.

There is a time and place. For example, knowing when it is appropriate to indulge in sexual behaviours, making sure you are contributing to society with a job...etc. But these things do not need to come at the cost of your inner child. If the inner child in you is neglected and you're not aware of your own soul, unbalance comes to exist and the unhealed trauma you have been carrying with you will transpire into forming bad habits, even disease, as it all stems from the dis-ease in your mind.

It's at this point that the adventure of life becomes one where we go through more hardships than are necessary. We suffer, from one necessity to another, in survival mode, with responsibilities that we are led to perceive as *reality*. We then interact with different personas & characteristic traits of others throughout life. As if it isn't bad enough that you are already letting your inner child and soul down, you then inevitably and regrettably let others down also, by not being true to yourself. This creates a vicious cycle that makes us feel like we're not good enough. Because, if you point the finger and have the belief that "this ain't good enough, that ain't good enough," eventually you will find that finger pointed right back at your own self.

It's ok; what matters is that we bring awareness to ourselves and stop conforming to others, what they expect and impose on us. More often than not, others mirror their insecurities onto us, so we lower our standards to theirs. The key is to always work on yourself, to put yourself first and align to the best version of you.

What if I was to tell you everything was always working out for you? That you should believe that things were always working out for you?

When you understand what it is you truly want (your soul's desires), you can see how everything is working out for you in your favour. It's all about your attitude. If you feel like nothing is going right for you, if you are beating yourself up (however you choose to do this), then guess what? You are putting yourself down. Pick yourself up. It's ok to slip up; fall by all means, but always be right there for yourself. Imagine your inner child falling and you now lending a helping hand. Help yourself!

You can choose to believe in magic and choose to be riding on a magical carpet throughout life, or you could think that is all nonsense. That's your choice. Although, let me tell you this...if you feel like you are never satisfied, you never will be. Perhaps you have been told that you act like the entire world revolves around you. Well, let me tell you right now that this is 100% a fact. This is your life, so own it! And if you are told that life is not supposed to be all fun and games, boy, have they got it wrong. Yes, it is, my friend, we are playing the game of life!

It is the satisfaction factor of life which we all came into existence for. Remember that chocolate ice cream analogy I spoke about before? We must be selfish with our own self. I don't mean the act of being selfish towards others. I mean that the act of being selfish with our own self is knowing what we truly want and what we are prepared to accept. It's in finding alignment with ourselves. When we connect to our inner child, we can actually, in turn, be selfless.

In hindsight, this is what I came to find out for myself only recently, that selfishness is no bad thing at all. You're free to express yourself. Selflessness and selfishness exist on a spectrum, and it is up to us to understand it and think of it, not in binary terms, but as one benefiting the other & vice versa. With that comes the knowledge of boundaries and what you are willing to stand for and put up with (I will get to that throughout this book).

So, let me ask you, what is it that you want out of life? What is it that you have to contribute to the world?

For therein lies your selfless service to the world, the magic of being on the receiving end of abundance, to feel the course of life surging through your body. It's the means by which you wake up in the morning. When we cooperate with who we are truly meant to be and what we truly want out of life, we give back to the Universe ten-fold and receive in kind.

Life truly is what you make of it. But of course, as children, we know this. It is only when the conditioning begins that we forget this fact.

In this story, I take you through the journey of my own conditioning, how it manifested throughout my life to my detriment and how I broke it, to get back to this truth. My hope is that you don't have to experience the hardships that I did, in order to get back to your own truth.

I would like to ask you to take a minute to stop for a moment, and answer these questions for yourself. Who am I? What is it that I want out of life? What does my heart truly desire and who do I want to be?

What would that look like for you and how would that make you feel? Begin by shutting yourself away from your world for a moment, with no distractions, and have a heart-to-heart with yourself, self-inquire! Take the time to ask yourself the questions above and then follow up with the questions below, whilst imagining living your perfect life. Be as elaborate and as descriptive as you can. Consider creating a blueprint of what you want your life to look like in the near future.

For example:

1- What are your thoughts, first thing, as you wake up?
2- Where would you live?
3- What does your house look like?
4- What car do you drive?
5- What time do you get up?
6- What is your routine and schedule like?
7- What do you have for breakfast?
8- What does the mundane stuff look like (sorting out the kids for school, for example)?
9- How about the rest of your day?
10- What do you do for work?
11- Are there any chores you need to do, or do you hire someone else to do them?
12- What do you have for lunch?
13- Who would you eat with?
14- What does your body look like and how do you feel about it?
15- Are you personally fulfilled?

16- What do you love about yourself?
17- Do you feel a sense of purpose?
18- What do you care about?
19- Have you got any hobbies?
20- Have you got any investments?
21- Are you still learning?
22- What are your attributes?
23- How many holidays would you like?
24- What do you dress like?
25- What do you smell like?
26- What is business like for you?
27- What do you offer your clients?
28- What are your clients like?
29- What are your relationships like?
30- What are your friendships like?
31- What is family life like?
32- What do you like about each other?
33- What do you do to bond?
34- What do you talk about over dinner?
35- What do you get up to in the evening?
36- Who would you do it with?
37- What would your thoughts be like, as you drop off to sleep?
38- What do you do over the weekends?
39- How do you feel about life and how do you feel

about yourself?

40- What are your prime emotions?

41- Finally, how does that compare to now? Is it worth your time to invest towards making that reality come true and what are you going to do about it?

Decide right now to envision your ideal life, your perfect life, if you will, and don't let my examples limit you from exploring more possibilities and outcomes. Be as elaborate and descriptive as you can, to suit the vision of your future and go as far as your imagination can stretch. From there, take action and be grateful for the ideas that bless you. This is how you can begin to connect and develop your relationship with your inner child and fantasise, as we once did as children, about how life may look, as we grow up. From there, you break your fantasy into theories and those theories are then broken down into goals that you then work up to and complete, to then lead your ideal life.

As adults, we have a habit of feeling like our deck of cards has already been shuffled and dealt and that is our fate. I know that's how I once thought. But this couldn't be further from the truth. At least, it's not once we start to use our imagination again and develop tunnel vision on those desires. Create something you can get excited about, first thing in the morning when you wake up, and smile about, as you head off to sleep. Think about it often. Do you recall what I said about creating neuron connections in the mind? By allowing yourself to envision your dreams in great detail, your subconscious begins to stretch awake and exercise, like a muscle, on how to make that dream a reality for you. Then you can start strategizing and, most importantly, begin to take action.

The world is your oyster, my friend, and the gift is you, in the form of a pearl, but only if you choose to believe it is so!

CHAPTER TWO: CHASING FREEDOM

My mum escaped from South Africa, with myself and my sister, when I was seven. All the shops and lamp posts, where we lived in Johannesburg, had posters up, warning all the white people to get out, while encouraging the black people to commit rape and murder.

To my surprise, in recent years, my parents disclosed that the move was also in attribution to our maid having begged my parents to get out of the area. She was starting to feel uncomfortable with everything that was going on and, as she was a black lady herself, she feared how picking up a young white kid from school looked within her own community. If it hadn't been for her and her connections, I would have most likely been kidnapped.

There was a rumour there was a witch doctor that had his eye on a white blonde-headed boy – me.

What a scary thought. I have since dug deeper, with research of my own, to understand the concept behind a witch doctor and the potential kidnap. I stumbled across an article with a similar story, where a young boy's torso was found, headless, and all the internal body parts had been removed. In those cases, it was suspected that the boys had been used as part of a ceremonial sacrifice. I discovered that the ritual was to do with some sort of sorcery, whereby the intention was to harvest the soul and energy, to strengthen the witch doctor's own gifts. A barbaric practice that many of us, myself included, find a strange idea to wrap our heads around.

I speculate that part of me, as a child, knew about the witch doctor and it was embedded in my subconscious, further feeding the belief that I wasn't safe in my own home. Reflecting, that revelation from my parents made my earliest memories of being locked up in the house even stranger. While my younger self felt ignored & abandoned, the man in me can now understand that our maid only had my best interest at heart and did care about my younger self. It's that wonderful paradox of life in action – when two truths are both a reality at once.

When we escaped South Africa, we arrived in Madeira, an island outside of Portugal and my native country. Not only was I a foreigner where I was born, but when we moved, I wasn't welcomed by the locals. I found myself getting picked on. "Go back to your country," they'd say, even though this was where my roots resided. I recall being surrounded by a group of kids, getting spat on, I can't say I had fun with that.

We had moved in with my grandparents, who had acres of land, growing all sorts of fruit, raising cattle and with its own river. I was free to roam the neighbourhood and I had many adventures here, especially as the sea was within walking distance. I well and truly explored all there was for me to exploit and tasted independence for the first time. How I must have driven all my loved ones mad, missing for hours on end! Despite being picked on, I have so many wonderful memories, especially from the summer.

My dad, however, had stayed behind in South Africa, to sell everything and make the transition over, which took about a year. Later, I would discover that he had held a gun to his head once or twice, as he felt so lonely, he missed us so much and felt like everything he had worked so hard for was crumbling around him. (To think that I would go on to experience something similar, as a grown man, is what we call a generational wound and repeating our parents' patterns is something we do, if we don't consciously work on our conditioning.)

The gun had been a means to protect himself, after he had been in the middle of an armed robbery, on several occasions. It's something I have a vague recollection of. I recall being in my mum's arms, while she was her crying, as she listened to a radio announcement broadcast from an overflying news helicopter, with news of my dad and others being held hostage.

I'm so grateful that he didn't use that gun against himself and eventually managed to join us.

With no dad around, it was up to my mum to make sure I was disciplined. All children need to learn how to be safe, while exploring their freedom, and my mum, like many others of her generation, used physical means. I remember being at a crowded shopping centre and she would prick me with a sewing pin lightly in the arse, to make sure I would behave quickly. It hurt and I had no clue what was going on, but I behaved. Looking back now, I can see and understand her point of view. In a foreign land where she didn't speak the language, a shock tactic was an effective way to get me to conform to "normal" behaviour.

My mum had also taken interest in a rubber sjambok she had found at the supermarket. How best to describe this to you? Imagine a horse-riding crop, long and thin. To me, it was intimidating, that was the whole point of it. I imagine my mum never dreamed of using it, bless her. But whether it was a shoe, a wooden spoon, or the sjambok, in the heat of the moment, I got a can of whoop ass. I recall that it hurt like hell, and if I'm honest, I never felt I warranted being punished with it, but it did the job, for sure.

I do admit, I did many naughty things, as I explored my

freedom, that I'm not proud of now. I can absolutely understand why my mum gave me a good old smack, when she found out I was stealing precious coins from my grandad and taking notes from my nan's purse. The fact that I would make a right meal out of it at the shops and chuck any leftover change down the drain to not get caught, is now ludicrous to me. Surely, it would have been wiser to hide the money, rather than throw it away, but we don't know what we don't know as children, right?

I had learnt, through other experiences, to come up with excuses. Like when we had dogs when I was younger and one day they disappeared. I loved them so much. They were my friends. When they disappeared, my parents gave me an excuse as to why, which I can't remember now. The excuse didn't make sense to me at the time and I was left heartbroken, devastated, and confused. I no doubt picked up on that example, as a way to justify any life events that made me feel like that in the future, coming up with excuses for my emotions and behaviour, too.

Later, in my teenage years, I would write a note any time I was naughty, expressing how genuinely sorry I was that I had hurt my parents' feelings. But often, as I began to have my own mind more and more, I would get into arguments with my parents – especially when Dad joined us again. I had my fair share of opinions and would defend myself. But that would turn into a confrontation and, before you know it, my dad would defend my mum, stating that I "didn't know what I was on about."

An expression that used to drive me nuts was when they would say to me, they "were not born yesterday" and that I was "imposing my thoughts" or that I was "full of shit." I would often leave the arguments feeling conflicted, as if I couldn't trust or believe in my own self. How I wish they would have said, "Interesting point of view. Are you able to see or consider another perspective?" Or at least I would have liked them to acknowledge my point or express what it made them think or feel, so I could build that level of connection and understanding deeper, with them and with myself. Instead, I was often left feeling humiliated and punished for expressing my feelings and questioning these overwhelming emotions. I never understood confrontation and found myself frustrated by the lack of compromise. Come to think of it now, I'd be driven mad when they would say "I had no respect." More so because, in those moments, I was starting to not have any for myself, let alone be offered the same.

This need to develop your own sense of identity, while being raised to be a good human, is possibly one of the hardest balancing acts parents must deal with, as their children grow up. I reflect now and think it's no wonder I feel physical discomfort and my anxiety goes through the roof, when I deal with confrontation. The inner child in me still longs for connection and seeks validation. My earliest memories associate this pain with confusion, excuses, and an inability to communicate effectively.

It left me feeling like no one understood me, a pattern that would continue, until I understood the root cause of it. To be honest, it's one I still struggle with, to this day. Self-mastery is a journey, and I learned this one quote well, "We never get things finished, we never get it done and there is no way that you can get it wrong. Our journey is more about getting on with it than waiting for the outcome of choice and allowing it to unfold as it is."

I am still working on being fully responsible for how I feel, no matter the circumstances, and to not pay any mind to the opinions of others. Their opinions are none of my business; they are free to think what they like. This is often where the parent-child relationship dynamic struggles, as we get older and search for our own truth, our own freedom, and our own way of being.

This is even harder when we reflect on things we have done that we aren't proud of and we resort back to that disciplined mindset our parents gave us. I have done so much that I am not proud of. But I reflect on the state of mind I was in at the time of those moments, and I'm reminded of another quote on enlightenment, "What you may know today is food for thought on tomorrow's epiphany."

The fact is, it is not the job of others, of parents, of maids, of locals, to know and understand you. It is your job to understand yourself. So, with that being said, I'll ask you the question I asked myself. Are you ready to bring back the earliest memories that you can recollect?

Using my experience of being locked indoors, and now knowing it was for a good reason, can you bring another perspective to your own memories? The good intentions and the negative repercussions? Can you see the logic of others in that moment? Or that of your own? Can you understand now what you might not have been able to, as a child? Can you see how those memories shaped your behaviour, as mine shaped me, to feel unseen, unheard, and unsupported?

Bring those memories to your mind's eye. Send each memory forgiveness and the compassion to understand that everyone around you did the best they knew how at the time, as you did, too. Call on your inner child and let it be known that, from now on, moving forward, here within you is safety. That you are loved and fully supported. That the older version of you is now progressively working on being loving, being kinder and being the friend you were always meant to be with your own self.

I would also highly recommend trying meditation, if you don't have a practice already. Although there are many variants, the benefits that meditation provides are great. One of those key benefits for me was that I began to practice discipline.

It takes a lot to remain still in the time you have given yourself to meditate. You may want to faff around, for example, or give up from boredom. In our daily lives, we are so easily distracted and the body fights to do what the mind suggests. Imagine yourself as a machine, if you will, where your mind is the computer and your subconscious is the program on the computer. Part of your programming will be happening on autopilot, which in real-world terms are the habits your body memorises. These become your default mode. For me, meditating was a means to break out of that unconscious programming. So, instead of doing what my body was naturally programmed to do, scratch my arse or move a leg, for example, meditating helped me to be mindful and strengthened me to be more in charge.

Another benefit of meditation, other than the art of discipline, is becoming consciously aware and getting familiar with yourself and therefore taking control of your internal programming. A lot of this is done in meditation, through focusing on the breath and silencing the mind.

What I mean by silencing the mind is to observe yourself. Don't get too involved with the narrative playing out in your head, as far as your thoughts are concerned. This is how you practice being present – by observing and being detached.

We're not taught *how* to feel, and we're hardly taught how to think and act consciously. I was surprised to discover that, from the moment a baby is formed in the womb and up until the age of six, children's minds are running on a suggestable program frequency. This is to prime their brain for how to survive in its environment.

Now, there are many of these frequencies that our brains run on, and there are different frequencies that can affect us on a daily basis – Delta, Theta and Alpha (although there are many others). What are frequencies, you might wonder? At the root of all our thoughts, emotions and behaviour, is the communication between neurons within our brains, otherwise known as brain waves, which produce electrical pulses that communicate with one another. This is what I mean by frequencies.

As we go through different states of awareness throughout the day, we are more suggestible at certain times to these frequencies than others, and as a result, release different chemicals throughout our nervous system, which affects our behaviour. The Theta frequency, for example, is used for hypnosis, to prime the mind to be more suggestible.

By meditating, we can also tap into these other frequencies and heightened states of awareness and, when combined with exploration of our emotions and thoughts of the mind, they allow us to run a simulation with ourselves. It is so interesting, because your subconscious cannot distinguish imagination from reality, so whatever you imagine in your mind, it believes to be true. It is with the frequency of Alpha where you can wander off in your own mind and begin to train it, going over a situation you are going to experience, an interview or an important meeting, for example. By running this simulation with yourself, you fire and wire those neuron connections in your mind and experience your ideal scenario, before it has even happened. You are only limited by your imagination.

Many studies have tracked athletes & high-performance individuals, using these methods to their advantage, as they train or prepare for their events or get ready for their day, before it has even begun.

There are so many variants, so far as frequencies are concerned. The frequency of 528 hz, for example, is the frequency of love. Bring the memories that trouble you to mind, as I asked you to do earlier, and listen to that frequency on the likes of a YouTube video. It will help you relax and feel love and compassion for those memories within your heart. If you find it difficult to feel those emotions, you might like to recite the Ho oponopono prayer and say this to yourself as I did: "I love you, I'm sorry, please forgive me, thank you." While you do this, breathe in and out, as if from the centre of your heart, with certainty that everything is ok, everything is always working out for you and that you are safe. Even if you experienced some traumatic things in your past, try to maintain the attitude that, if you could turn back the hands of time, you wouldn't change a thing.

Use the information I have shared with you and practice being present. What does it feel like to be grateful? Feel into what "it's just so awesome to be you" means to you. Cut out the need for others validation, those conditions & circumstances you believe have to be in place in order to receive validation, and give it to yourself, regardless. Hone in on being able to turn that on at a flick of a switch & you will be able to unconditionally offer love and compassion to yourself and the world at large.

CHAPTER THREE: EXPLORING SEXUALITY

Part of finding your freedom and knowing your own mind as you grow up is exploring sexuality. We are all exposed to it much younger than society says we should be. Kids are curious creatures, and I am often amazed at how many of us had young sexual experiences that we feel shamed into not talking about, because we aren't "of age" and don't feel comfortable talking about it in the first place. I wonder how different many of us might feel, if this subject was widely open for discussion.

On one hand, I have children myself and, while I can imagine talking with my daughter about this would be uncomfortable, I am well aware from my own experience how children play "Mummies and Daddies." I'm sure children naturally put two and two together and gather from observation the difference in their anatomy, for one. And I appreciate that sex education can be a touchy subject. No parent wants to introduce it to their children in the sense of feeling like they're influencing them to partake in something they aren't ready for.

However, here is food for thought. Wouldn't you say

that we have the responsibility to teach them how they were created, to teach them about what it means to love and what it means to conceive a child of their own, when attraction becomes part of their biology, beyond just the "wait for marriage and kids" speech most of us got (and didn't listen to)? I think teaching them the foundations of wanting to create a family, and how sacred this act is, is a beautiful place to start from, but we often leave out the details and realities, in order to preserve their innocence. But if they are already watching and wondering, curious children without answers will then go and seek them out for themselves! Far better that we educate them truthfully, don't you think? We have an opportunity here, to give them a wonderful introduction to what it means to love another, but also what it means to love your own self, and maintain your self-respect and self-worth, even as you explore your sexuality. To teach them how to allow for the best outcome in any situation regarding sex and to bear in mind peer pressure and boundary setting, too.

When I was nine, I recall my excitement at going through all my dad's VHS tapes. They were in one of the boxes brought over from South Africa and, being a right nosy so-and-so, I found myself rummaging through it. I came across some gold! I loved getting lost for hours in action films, with the likes by Jean-Claude Van Damme,

Sylvester Stallone and Arnold Schwarzenegger.

One day, however, I came across a tape that had most likely been forgotten about. It was a porno tape. I was shocked. I knew it was naughty, though I don't remember my parents ever giving me the sex talk. The video contents were quite graphic. I suppose part of me instinctively knew this wasn't the sacred act of sex between two people, the respectful, self-worth version, but something...dirtier.

I ended up hiding it after watching it. Funnily enough, the tape ended up disappearing again. But the damage had already been done, and at nine years old, I had been influenced by sexual content.

The only other time I had experienced anything sexual before that was when I was around four or five years old, in South Africa, though it was nothing like the tape. I remember having a neighbour who was the same age as me, and we were playing in his bedroom, the two of us experimenting with each other. How did that come about, I wonder? Was I under his influence? Was he under mine? Were we acting out something either one of us saw our parents do? I imagine I'm not far off from the truth. Either way, what I do know is that it made me uncomfortable later in life and gave me nightmares of anxiety and confusion, growing up.

After I found the tape, a similar thing happened with

one of my childhood friends. We were around the same age and, having been exposed to unadulterated content early on, it seemed convenient for us to play out these scenes by hiding away, kissing, and playing Mummies and Daddies. Our underdeveloped minds were trying to process what we had been exposed to, but thankfully our underdeveloped bodies wouldn't recreate the act. Though I will never forget what she said to me that day; "Do it like my Uncle does it." I feel incredibly uneasy even writing those words now.

As a consequence, I started experimenting. One time by letting my dog lick my penis and another time playing around with my Mum's dildo. I was alone in the house whilst she went to run errands. How I found it, only the child back then knows, but I have a suspicion I was being nosy once again. I ended up putting it in my mouth, before trying to insert it in my bum.

I even tried to look up my great-grandmother's skirt once, much to my embarrassment and shame.

When I was around ten, I would follow around an older lad I looked up to. I wanted to be just as cool as he was, having no idea what he was capable of at the time. One day, he, another boy and I went for a walk up to the hills and into the woods, cracking jokes and messing about when we stopped. The older lad took out his penis and started to play with himself, encouraging us to do the same. I now can see that he was grooming us and wanted to have sex with us, but I refused. I was really uncomfortable with the whole situation, especially when he proceeded to have sex with the other boy.

This wasn't the first or the last time something like this happened. Another boy from the bottom of town and I used to walk home the same way. Midway through the walk one day, he took me with him around a corner by a farm and started masturbating, before he ejaculated on the floor in front of me. I found it funny and weird, but thought no more of it. As I write this now, I feel uncomfortable with the thought that he likely wanted the younger me to act on him as well.

As you might imagine, this is all very uncomfortable for me to share. As a man looking back now, what comes to mind after healing these memories that have plagued me is this; I was just an innocent, curious child, acting out what I had seen on the VHS tapes and wanting to understand sexual anatomy, why girls had other parts, and trying to fit in with the older boys. More to the point, I knew no better, trying to wrap my mind around something I wasn't old enough to comprehend yet.

I always wondered why I was uncomfortable around men growing up. I also wondered why I was so withdrawn, anti-social and felt like I was off-key. For one, I didn't have a ''normal'' relationship with my father growing up, as he wasn't around that much. We didn't hang out. Add that to these experiences that I just shared and it's no wonder I felt uncomfortable. So much so that my child brain blocked out parts of those memories, of other boys pleasuring themselves around me and that instance of seeing another boy getting penetrated, until I was writing this book.

From my understanding now, the neuron patterns I would have started developing in these situations were part of my "freeze" response. A means to protect myself in situations where I did not feel safe. But until I recognised this response, it continued as a loop, a story, in my head.

Unfortunately, it resulted in me somewhat shutting off from the world, withdrawn and numb. For our reptilian brain, the one responsible for the freeze response and the survival aspect of our mind, concentrates on all the negatives, rather than the best of outcomes, especially when trauma is involved.

What is the reptilian brain, you might ask? I like to think of our brains as lego. Along the evolutionary line, our minds evolved from the reptilian brain – the first piece of lego. In fact, if you were to dissect the human brain, you would see the same structure as the reptilians at the centre of our brain. Only, as we've evolved (by my own analogy), we've added extra pieces of lego and our brain has become a more sophisticated piece, with many elements to study.

This "freeze" response and my lack of being able to communicate with anyone about sexual acts only made me more insecure about my earlier childhood memories. Why didn't I discuss this with a parent? Why don't kids ever come forward? Is it just shame? Embarrassment? Fear of judgement? Because we, as adults, aren't completely transparent with them, so they aren't with us? All I can tell you is, the guilt from my earliest memories, having hidden the VHS tape and the other experiences, contributed to hiding all aspects of myself in later life, which kept me in the shame loop spiral.

Looking back, it's clear to see where the communication problems started. Breeding shame around a subject and never disclosing the events that happen to you is never healthy. How different it would have been for me, if I had only been brave enough to express myself and talk to an adult. But it was only as I began writing this book, for the first-time self-inquiring, that I addressed the wounds that triggered these thoughts and feelings over and over again.

Instead, throughout my teens, I felt like I had a dark secret. It burdened me to think that, if anyone knew about these experiences, they would mock me for being gay. How did I even make that association that being gay was a dark secret? I suppose, given that I had a Mum and a Dad, I knew this as the "norm" for sexual couples and I instinctively felt like homosexuality was not for me, but that is my own personal experience. It was these experiences and thoughts that made me uncomfortable around blokes. I didn't trust them, given what I had been exposed to.

I recall when I first started experimenting with myself in private. Having felt aroused one evening when I was locked away in my bedroom, I was surprised to feel my penis erect. I started pleasuring myself and, to my shock, had an orgasm, which felt good! But in my haste for more, I wanted to achieve another orgasm after another. I masturbated over and over again, until I could ejaculate no more and to the point where my penis and balls would ache the next day.

How is this something you even discuss with your parents, as a teen? I can't imagine talking about it with my mum. Though it would have been nice with Dad to at least talk about the beautiful girl that had taken a liking to me and made advances.

I'll never forget her. I've always regretted how awkward I was at the time, knowing that she liked me. She was beautiful. She had blonde hair, she was confident, she knew what she liked, and she went after it...which was me, at the time. I wasn't shy (I don't think) and, despite my lack of communication, I had a flair for life and was cheeky.

She came knocking at my door one afternoon after school, but my parents said I was too young to be dating at sixteen, which made me feel like a bit of a loser, and off she went. I made an excuse that day, but arranged to meet her another time. If only my parents had known that, by this point, I had been sexually experimenting for several years, without them knowing!

The next time we met, she and I hung out with another friend of ours. Together, we found an abandoned boat on an industrial estate and my mate dared us to go inside, so we did. Inside, she offered to give me a blowjob. I'll never forget how she looked at me and, for the life of me, I can't recall why I rejected her, although I imagine it might have been anxiety.

I regret not kissing her, I regret not allowing her to indulge with me. I had started by now to grow accustomed to hating my own behaviour. The way I carried myself was awkward and I felt like I was not worthy of her attention. I was not shy, but I *was* insecure. To top it off, I felt like my penis was small, perhaps because I was comparing it to what I had seen in adult movies and the older lads in the neighbourhood from the past. Feeling like my own worst nightmare, she soon sacked me off, disappointed and no doubt fed up with my frigidness. This would cause my insecurities and shyness in this area to develop even further.

My parents were right. I wasn't ready, despite my experimentation. And my experience with the girl just piled on more embarrassment, shame, and lack of confidence that I couldn't talk about with anyone.

As children and young teens, we get so fed up with being told what is "right and wrong" by adults, even as we watch them contradict themselves, with the likes of VHS tapes and dildos and whatever else. Either way, we don't know what we don't know, right?

If only the communication channel had more freedom and less shame, I might not have had sexually repressed experiences that would later come back to bite me in the bum.

What are you ashamed about from childhood, even now, for that matter? How can my story help you to shed light on your own experiences? Feel free to write it out and spend time sitting with it, feeling it. Go on, give it a go.

One of the biggest gifts you can give yourself is to self-inquire, take it from me. Try to do so without any judgement. Roll your shoulders back, put your chest out, pretend you are opening up your heart wide and shed light on it. For any judgement you hold will only create further obstacles for you.

The aim here is detachment. Try to let it go, give it a good cuddle & cradle that image of the memory with love, as we practiced in the last chapter. Give it care, but don't pay any mind to how different you wish it had been. However it hurts, let it be what it was and fully feel into it; this is the only way to truly let it go.

The best thing you can do is come to a state of compassion and forgiveness for yourself and for those who might have contributed to the memory. Repeat after me, "We know what we knew at the time and so it was." Now let it be. This is what you call an affirmation, something I'll come to in another chapter.

After saying that affirmation, imagine freezing the memory in your mind's eye. Put it into a box and imagine closing that box. Send it away and see it disappear before your eyes, with the intention that it no longer serves you and it does not need to burden you anymore. Repeat this exercise, if necessary, as I did and, after a while, you may just start to feel good about it, should you choose to believe in the box dissolving for good.

This exercise reminds me of a story about a man who was carrying a rucksack of all his belongings, down a long stretch of road. Along the way, after miles and miles at some point, he came across another man with a spring in his step, who was whistling. The man who was whistling noticed the man with the rucksack struggling.

"Why are you carrying all that with you, mate, any purpose?" he asked.

"Yes," the other man responded. "This is pretty cool, check it out, I found it along my way here. The other stuff is things I've also collected over the years, and the rest of the stuff are belongings my family passed down to me..."

"But why carry it when you are clearly struggling? Why not let it go and be free, my friend? You will be so much more at peace."

My encouragement is that we all do the same thing.

One final exercise that might help you in this area is as follows. Get a notepad out and list the name of every person you can think of, whom you feel has done you wrong at some point in your life. At the end, with an open mind, go through each name and put your right hand to your heart and say, "I now understand that you knew no better at the time. I now release the burden that I carry with me in your name and image, with forgiveness, as I wish you all the best."

I reached almost three hundred names when I did this exercise. Each time I repeated it, I felt lighter. I now feel no emotional attachment towards any of those three hundred names. It feels fantastic not to have any emotional tie with the past, so try it. Look inside your rucksack.

CHAPTER FOUR: BULLIED FOR NOT BEING THE "STATUS QUO"

Remember that blonde girl in the abandoned boat and my best friend? I was returning home from holiday and looking forward to seeing him. But the day we hung out, he asked me if I liked sloppy seconds. I had no idea what he meant, and he wouldn't explain himself, but I later found out, when I had been away on holiday, he had been messing around with the blonde girl behind my back.

When I found out, I felt empty inside, let down, humiliated. I was so confused. It didn't add up; how could he? Deep down, I knew this wasn't right, that friends didn't do this to one another. He lived across the road from me, so we hung out mostly every day and played games, mucked about outside and generally always had a good time. Not once had we fallen out or come to bad terms, until now. I didn't trust him anymore, and he didn't reach out to mend our friendship, either. I imagine he knew that he had crossed a line.

But my boundaries were non-existent. We say we teach

kids boundaries, but when it comes to finding their own circle of friends, their self-respect and self-worth...well, that we all too often learn the hard way.

I had no self-respect, for one, and I wasn't aware of my self-worth. I felt like there was something about me, although it wasn't something I could measure. Others couldn't get the measure of me either, so I ended up getting picked on a lot.

I didn't want to fight. But I started to hate myself more for not defending myself, sometimes so upset with myself that I didn't fight back and let anyone put their hands on me and hurt me. I recall once or twice getting into a fight, but it was as if my body shut down on me and I held back.

With no self-respect or self-worth, I later ended up befriending another "best friend" who was toxic for me. I can't recall what happened the first time we got into an altercation at school, but I remember him punching me on the nose and leaving me bleeding and embarrassed, in front of everyone. I can see now that I was an easy target, one which would inflate his ego and his own social status. The fact we remained friends for many years, to the point that our friendship didn't end until I found out he was making advances on the mother of my child, years later, goes to show how little I thought of myself and how that pattern would continue for a long time yet.

He was not the only boy to physically "put me in my place." On a walk around the park with the blonde girl (before I knew she was fooling around with my best friend), we came across another boy in my year. We were all around sixteen at the time and I always used to find this guy a little intimidating. I was never comfortable around him; he wasn't particularly nice. He would belittle anyone he felt superior to, and he had a bit of a reputation for being quick to give you a smack. On this walk, he was with a friend of his and they were laughing as they approached us.

"You get two choices," he told me. "Either I punch you in the stomach or you're getting one in the face."

Out of fear, I reluctantly responded by choosing my stomach. Why didn't I say neither? I felt like I had no choice, but I was proud of my abs and knew I could tense vigorously, to withstand the blow and stand up to him. Then bam, I was sucker-punched, right in the gut. I walked away, trying to remain as normal as possible.

"Are you ok?" the girl asked me.

"It's no bother," I responded, though I could hardly get the words out. I was out of breath and in agony, but I put on a brave face and composed myself with a tough exterior. Inside, I felt humiliated, distraught, and embarrassed. I swiftly made my excuses and went back home.

I tried to make sense of it all by comparing humans with animals. The playground started to look a little like the jungle to me, with its own hierarchy. One in which I couldn't defend myself because I had no experience.

The dreams I had at night didn't help. In my nightmares, I would try to protect myself from bullies, but I couldn't swing, nor could I flee. My legs wouldn't carry me, I froze, and when I needed to raise my voice to yell, not an ounce of air would escape my lips. All I would feel was the frustration at not being able to move my mouth...

Knowing what I know now about our neural processes, I know that, in cases of extreme stress, or life-endangering circumstances, we go into what is called fight or flight mode, which is all in correspondence to the sympathetic nervous system. In my case, I was reliving some of my social experiences within my dreams, whereby I needed to defend myself. When this response is activated, you either fight or flee, but in my dream, I could do neither. Instead, I would withdraw. In freeze mode, I was incapable of making a response and would freeze, like a rabbit in the headlights.

I was starting to feel like I was part of a concrete playground jungle, in which case I was the prey, and the predators were out to get me. But why? Was it because I was the threat? I was getting picked on and usually for no reason, other than just for being me. I'll admit, I was loud and cheeky. I also, in my desperation to fit in and without a doubt to make my own stance socially, picked on others. But I never intended to harm or bully anyone. Were these kids the same? Were we all just trying to find our place in the hierarchy? Was it all just a matter of self-respect and self-worth?

Even so-called friends seemed to be against me. One group came knocking for me and I distinctly remember I had this pair of shoes I was really proud of, sitting outside on the front porch. They were navy in colour, smart, and had writing over them, like a newspaper press. When I went to greet my friends, I noticed saliva on the inside of one of the shoes, as if someone had spat in them. I confronted everyone, but they all laughed and denied it. I knew one of them had spat in them. Looking back, my self-respect and self-worth was so negligible as to be non-existent, so that even my "friends" at the time mirrored it back to me.

I never felt safe; perhaps that was in part because I was foreign and perhaps it was in part because I was hiding my true self. It was as if I was a trembling mess on the inside, as if I didn't know how to behave or how to be myself. I felt different, alien. It didn't help that this was all amplified, after learning that I was dyslexic at school. Now, on top of everything, I felt as though I was incompetent, in relation to everyone else.

So, I ran from myself, and this manifested on two occasions when I felt I had to run for my life.

One time, in the evening as I was heading back home, I came across two lads who I asked to borrow a lighter from. We got to talking and the conversation soon changed tone. Who did I think I was and why was I talking like I was black? I told them I was born in South Africa and that might be the reason why. They didn't like that. They wanted to kick my head in and chased after me. Luckily, I was quick on my feet and outran them.

The second time, I was again walking – this time to a party. I was wearing these fresh cream shoes I had just brought that day, to match my outfit. I saw a group of boys shouting at a lad; it seemed as if they were after him. To my surprise, they acknowledged me by confirming to one another that I was also South African. With that, they went after me, yelling, "Get that foreign scum!" I'll never forget this, as those new shoes were a little loose and I was unable to really give way and leg it. I had to crow my toes in, in order to run as fast as I could.

I was a long way from home, but I realised I wasn't far off from a friend's house. I ended up running to her front door, banging as hard and as fast as I could. Luckily for me, there was a response and I hid inside. Her father ended up going outside to see what the hell was going on and managed to defuse the situation. I was so frightened to go outside that night that I begged for a lift home.

These were not the only times I had to run from confrontation. I was running from myself, my lack of self-respect and self-worth chasing me, like shadows in the form of bullies. And so, I ran towards the status quo, in the hopes of escaping them.

It didn't help that I hung around with the wrong crowd. My friends at the time got a kick out of treating others badly and banter was rife. I guess we were all dealing with our own insecurities and projecting them out onto each other, to protect our own individual false sense of security.

Being sensitive didn't help me. I didn't trust anyone. Things were either done behind my back to degrade me or, when they were done in front of me, I felt uncomfortable. Like the time I stayed over with a friend who threw a house party, only to wake up in the morning, to see him watching animal porn on the telly, while his girlfriend made us breakfast. She then sat down with us and watched it as well; that was awkward!

To avoid any further confrontation, I learned to keep my mouth shut.

I started smoking weed instead. It was one of the few things we could do, growing up, and my friends loved it.

We would have a smoke and walk about; there wasn't anything else to really do. That's what we told ourselves, as teenagers. The productivity intelligence we had amongst ourselves wasn't particularly high, even before we smoked the weed.

One night, I was smoking a joint out of my bedroom window, before going to sleep. As I was lying there in the pitch black, with the ambient light coming from outside through the window, I was staring at a picture frame, when the room looked as if it was starting to cave in on me. I felt something grabbing hold of my throat and noticed that I was unable to move when I tried. Then I heard the most sinister voice I have ever heard in my head.

"Sell me your soul."

My instinct was to pray to God.

My parents were Catholics, and I was raised as one also, attending church every Sunday and part of the church choir ever since I was nine years old. So, I closed my eyes and prayed.

"Please help me."

Just like that, my throat felt lighter, I could move, and the walls retreated out from around me and back to normal. I was terrified and had no way of making sense of it all.

I have since pondered on this experience and how my

life could have gone. Was conforming to the status quo the selling of my soul that demon voice talked about? Now, I know there were two ways my life could have unravelled. One where I might have turned out cold and narcissistic. The other – the path I eventually chose – where I would be in touch with my emotions and be faithful to my inner child and my highest self.

I came to this realisation when I became aware that all I was trying to do was fit in. My social circle was always in trouble. If it hadn't been for the strong moral Catholic values my parents instilled in me, I might have wanted to build a harder reputation for myself and be one of the lads that didn't give two shits about anyone and took what they could get. I might have sold drugs and been quick to lash out at anyone that crossed me. Admittedly, I looked up to those lads, at the time. They were fearless and had a reputation not to be messed with. I, on the other hand, was insecure and vulnerable – it's no wonder I admired that.

While, now and again, I was getting into fights, I actually secretly wanted to avoid confrontation at any cost. I had hate within me, but it wasn't so much at the world. Instead, I hated myself. My insecurities were unbearable to live with. To make it worse, I couldn't help imagining myself through the eyes of others and what they thought of me.

It never crossed my mind to consider what I thought about myself and what it would take to care about myself. Instead, I sought validation and measured myself, based on my experience with others. Some of us are led to believe that self-care means moisturising your skin and brushing your teeth. I didn't know how to look after myself outside of that, to be honest.

Which is why walking meditations, as an adult man, were a real turning point for me. Before this, I hadn't ever gone for a purposeful walk. That is what a walking meditation is. In the first lockdown, I would walk for hours. The first time I did it, I noticed I wasn't grounded in myself. My self-talk started coming into play and I hated the way I perceived and talked to myself.

I imagine we have all had moments when we are walking away from someone and get the feeling that we're being watched. For whatever reason, we find ourselves stumbling or feeling funny about the way we walk suddenly. I know I have.

So, I tried this exercise – feel free to do the same when you have a chance. Next time you go out for a walk, try walking with purpose, like you belong. Take your time with each step and walk in the way that you would like to carry yourself. Walk tall and proud.

The first time I did this, I noticed I slouched a bit. I

imagine that, over the years, my body curled inwards, as if to say I had pretty much given up on myself. How would it feel to stand up tall, I wondered? To my surprise, good posture instantly made me feel proud and it felt good.

I also noticed that, when I walked, I kind of stumbled around and swept my feet, as well. I began wondering how it would feel to take each step as if I belonged. I then took each step off the ground in a straight line.

I then paid attention to how I carried my body, and with that, how my arms moved accordingly, in sequence to each step, with a sense of awareness. It was as if I could see myself as a third person, observing myself from outside of my body.

I noticed something else interesting, too, how I acted when I passed passers-by. I was looking down, as if not to bring any attention to myself. So, I began to make eye contact and I imagined my presence as a blessing and smiled. There was, I discovered, something so warming in meeting a stranger for the first time and, in turn, receiving a smile.

In short, being mindful as to how I walked, carried, and perceived myself made me more confident *in* myself. Give it a try next time you go on a walk. If you're anything like me, within time, you will find your own confidence soaring and, in general, start improving how you carry yourself.

CHAPTER FIVE:
CAVING INTO PEER PRESSURE

As a consequence of having moved around a lot, and not having lots of friends, I had turned into someone who felt like they had to fit in. At school, I was the class clown, always acting silly or drawing. Because I didn't take school seriously, I ended up doing really badly. I never paid any notice to my homework and my parents used to despair over me. However, they didn't help me manage my time better, to allow for homework or make sure that I did it. Perhaps, they were trying to teach me responsibility. Now, I wish they had made me aware of the bigger picture, to realise I was investing in my future.

But you can't tell teenagers anything; they know it all, don't they?

I'll never forget the day we were all collectively at school together, to receive our GCSE grades. There was joy, laughter and, now and then, you saw the odd face that showed no emotion. I was one of the latter. I was quivering on the inside, not looking forward to opening my envelope, because I knew I had nothing to show for it, not like the others, who could show how many A's they had received. Upon opening the letter, I was met with disappointment.

The penny dropped and time froze. If I was able to draw in a superpower at will, I would have been out of there like Flash. I was embarrassed, I felt like a failure, disheartened, and convinced the damage was irreversible. To me, it was a clear indication of how worthless and how intellectually incapable I was, which did my self-esteem no good. What a vicious cycle our beliefs about ourselves are.

I had started to notice, too, how some of my peers were not of my stature. They were well-presented, happy, successful and in better classes than I was. Meanwhile, I hung around with 'the idiots', so to speak, who smoked weed and had something to prove, by throwing their weight around and mouthing off.

I had nothing to celebrate and was not looking forward to going home that day. I imagined I would be met by my parents' disapproval, a muttering of, "I knew you would have done badly," which is exactly what happened, when I reluctantly showed them my grades. My parents didn't know I was struggling to fit in; they were preoccupied with their own lives. A little bit of compassion & understanding about what was going on in the background, rather than looking at the face value of the consequences and results, would have gone a long way in helping.

Instead, after disappointing them, I locked myself in my room for the rest of the day, feeling like a lost cause, playing Xbox, and trying to numb away any feeling I had of discontent and shame. At least I didn't kick off, slam doors and what not. Instead, I went on some downtime and switched off — a healthier coping mechanism, I'm sure you might agree.

Fast forward a few months and I had the opportunity to make it right. My dad had arranged for me to go for an interview at a local college, for a position in the graphics design programme, seeing as it was what I had told the teacher I really wanted to do, after leaving high school. The teacher noted that my grades were awful and that I wouldn't be guaranteed a position to study graphic design, but I was adamant that I would excel. The teacher took a liking to me, and both he and my dad felt confident I would be an ideal candidate.

I was given the position.

"Son, this is your chance to put right what you failed at school," my dad told me.

I was so relieved. I couldn't believe I would get to do something I was passionate about, that was creative. My dream of drawing Dragon Ball Z characters was going to become a real career!

It was compulsory to buy an iMac for the course and some other pricey software, which my dad took out a loan for. He didn't even hesitate. After having a conversation with me, to make sure we both knew what I was getting into and the responsibility I had, I promised him there was no way I was going to mess this up. I would make new, better friends.

I was going to study to be a graphic designer!

My first day attending college was exciting. This was another world I was stepping into; the possibilities were endless. Walking down the yard on that first day, I heard music from a distance. I walked towards where the noise was coming from and found a bunch of lads, rapping and beatboxing. I approached them with amazement and curiosity and they, in turn, greeted me with welcome arms and answered all my questions. I was one of two lads who approached them in fascination, and we all laughed at how cool and fun this hobby of theirs was.

From then on, I met up with them at any opportunity I had. One of the lads in the group was in the same class as me, so we became fast friends. He introduced me to all of his mates, and I wanted to be just like them. I started to dress like them, I started to use the same slang they did, and I started trying to colour coordinate my shoes with my t-shirts. At any opportunity, I would buy new clothes, so I could dress accordingly, to fit in.

I started to write lyrics to rap; I couldn't wait to share them, but was always a nervous mess, my hands sweaty, and I would freeze before performing them. I wanted to so badly, but I didn't have the courage. I feared making a fool of myself. It used to kill me, that thought of making a fool of myself. I was still clearly constantly insecure and refusing to let go of it.

Still, I called myself Slick Mc, which was welcomed by my new friends and their friends. I had found my identity. I was one of the cool kids. I finally fitted in. I belonged.

But my promise to my dad was starting to fall apart. Now, all I cared about was writing song lyrics, drawing graffiti, and smoking joints on my way home, spending the rest of the day making music on my iMac. I ended up failing once again, as all my homework was submitted at the last minute. We were supposed to spend hours researching and writing articles about our design, which lost me my grades, even though my designs were good. I was confused by how I could have done so badly, when the designs were good, but energy flows where attention goes and mine was firmly invested into fitting in.

Weed was cool in my new crowd, too, and I started finding porn on my iMac later in the evening, so I locked myself away in my bedroom most nights. Weed and porn went hand in hand. I went from enjoying the recreational aspect of smoking weed to identifying the aphrodisiac element it offered. I started to fantasise about what it would be like to have a girlfriend. And so, my attention diverted even further away from my studies.

I came across a site, where you could make an account and make friends with other people online and I started talking to a girl I fancied. The conversation was always sexual, and I enjoyed asking if she enjoyed this, that or the other, based on what I had seen on the porn videos I was into and wanted to experience. I was really excited when we exchanged numbers. I'll be honest, there was something about her. She had this cute look about her, but with a naughty glint in her eye. That's exactly what I liked about her. The first time we spoke, the conversation on the phone lasted late into the evening and I hoped no one overheard us.

"Do you like giving blowjobs?" I remember asking.

"Yes," she replied.

My jaw must have hit the floor and I was erect from the excitement of it all.

As the conversation came to an end, we decided to meet up on Friday night, after college. I ended up going over to her house for the night, where we had a drink, smoked some weed, and had sex. Leaning back, smoking a joint while she gave me a blowjob, was like nothing the teenage boy in me could imagine. Even the thought of her stepdad being in the house, the fact his bedroom was next door, wasn't enough to put us off in the heat of the moment, while we were intoxicated with drugs, alcohol, and each other.

But it was more than that. I enjoyed the flow of conversation; there was banter and we got on really well. We shared great times together. I introduced her to my mates, and she was welcomed, since she was just as crazy as we were. She made me laugh, and we used to party wildly together. On the weekends, I would drive us to house parties, where we would take a few ecstasy pills. We would have a drink, smoke some weed, listen to music, and crack jokes with each other, late into the night. We developed our own little jokes, like when we were really wasted, she would hold my penis for me and help me draw Mickey Mouse on the walls, whenever I went for a piss. I started to fall in love with her, because she complimented my goofy side.

Aside from that, I loved kissing her! It was the most amazing thing ever to snog. That's what I liked the most about being in a relationship. That and having someone that I could count on; she had my back, as I had hers. Did I mention the sex? That's how I ultimately fell in love. My desire for intimacy transpired through sex and replicated my longing for a connection.

It wasn't until recently that I came to realise I was using

sex as a means to feel good about myself, for a release. Even in the comfort of a relationship, I felt that's how love was supposed to be expressed, through that level of intimacy. If I hadn't been offered it, I would question if she loved me.

It took me a little while to understand how I was investing my energy. Especially as a single man throughout this book writing process. Why was I masturbating? Why was I seeking multiple partners to have sex with?

I learned I was seeking quick gratification, which left me still feeling empty afterwards. I was still unsatisfied and unfulfilled, because I was lacking that level of intimacy with myself, with little passion for my own life. From that day moving forward, I made a promise to myself to never indulge with my own self or seek out sexual experiences for pleasure. I instead chose to practice self-discipline, harness dignity, and concentrate on my life. To use my sexual energy, instead, for getting creative with how I can improve my life.

We often seek passion from others, but what of our passion for ourselves? My days were spent wasting time. I needed to fall in love with the realisation of what it means to be alive, and how to make the most of life.

Especially when I started to feel like I would be far better off dead, that it wouldn't matter if I didn't wake up from my sleep the next morning. That was sad to admit to myself. What do you do with a grieving answer like that? The following: you must have something that you believe in. Figure out what you're passionate about, what your purpose is, your reason for being. What are you willing to fight for? Your 'why you wake up in the morning', that exists deep in your soul. You must be unapologetically you and show off your talents. You have to say, "OK, world, this gift is from me to you."

When I was writing this book, I reflected on everything I felt went wrong in my life. I put *everything* under the spotlight. I looked at what was going on in the present time. I felt like everything was going wrong and thought that the days ahead of me looked no different, either. By now, I'd lost count of how many times I let myself and others down, until this realisation. What are you going to do about it, I thought? I started to panic. It all seemed out of my control. Then it dawned on me that I was paying attention to everything I felt was "going wrong", instead of focusing on what was going right for me! Where you place energy is where your focus goes, right? The only alternative was to switch it up.

So, I started to reflect on everything that was going well for me. Right here and now, what did I have to be grateful for? I reached for a pen and paper and wrote down everything in the present moment and expressed how grateful I was right then. I then had an idea. What would it be like to have my dream life come to pass in reality? What would it feel like? So, I began to have some fun with that.

I wrote, for example, "I am so happy and grateful now that I am healthy and in great shape. My thoughts about myself are growing more positive every day and my confidence is soaring. I am so happy and grateful now that I am met with unexpected joys and prosperous opportunities that come to me with open arms. I am so happy and grateful now that I am continuously inspired. That I, too, inspire another fellow human being. That I am motivated to always be the better version of myself today than the version I was the day before. With that, I am so happy and grateful now that I am always reaching new heights, knowing wholeheartedly that everything is always working out for my highest good and that of all others."

This is what you call an affirmation.

There is a saying in the law of attraction community, "Without coordinates set into the GPS system, there is no destination to move forward towards." It's all very well, saying you're going east, for example, but you could be heading to where you think is east and then arrive at east, only to find yourself back where you started...nowhere near the east you wanted to be at all!

These affirmations are your starting coordinates.

I want to give you an insight into how I came about writing out these affirmations and how you yourself can write out your own and apply them, suited to your own circumstances and what you want out of life.

You have the power and the ability, right now inside of you, to solve every problem & to deal with every challenge that life throws at you. Your mind is a powerful tool and it's always working to give you the results you expect of reality. If you look at life as one of scarcity and limited possibilities, that is exactly what you're going to get. However, if you look at life and view yourself as having so much potential, that you are limitless and unstoppable, well, your mind will find a way to make that happen instead.

You've got to ask yourself if what you want for yourself is the same as what you expect. The people that we view as successful are no different than you and I. What separates them from the rest is how they view themselves and their lives in their own minds.

You've got to know what you want and fully expect to get it. You've got to take the necessary steps to bring it about and you must know that there will be challenges along the way. And you must know that you can face them, because you have done it before in the past.

With that being said, what can you write down in present tense that you can recite for when you are feeling like you're facing defeat? Go so far as to have these affirmations written out and pinned in your room, where you can read them every day. Write ones that can make you feel empowered, regardless of what you have going on or what comes your way. Have it up on your wall beside you, where you go to bed; your reason why you want to wake up in the morning, right there in front of you. Read it often and burn it into the back of your mind!

CHAPTER SIX: LIKE ATTRACTS LIKE

The more time I spent with this girl I fancied, the more I started paying attention to what she was like as a person. The thing that really got to me was that she took no pride in her bedroom. It was a mess; clothes everywhere, dry ketchup on the bedside unit and a plate on the floor that had been there a week ago. The floor clearly hadn't been vacuumed in months. It gave me the impression she was a bit scatty. It made me start to pay attention to the details and observe more about her and, subsequently, our relationship.

The first time I mentioned her predisposition for mess, she got defensive and we ended up in an argument. More accurately, I got my head bitten off. And like I had with my parents when they confronted me, I retaliated by defending myself. I felt I was only trying to express an observation, to understand her better. For her, it must have seemed like an attack on her character. In the heat of the argument, the purpose of the comment got lost in translation.

The more defensive I got, the more the facts got exaggerated. Her room was a shit hole. For me, that showed she took no pride and didn't care. But from there, I let it bleed into her not caring about what I thought and therefore she couldn't care less about how I felt, either.

The good times were great, but as far as accountability for each other – we had none. And we didn't know how to create that healthily with each other, so we rolled with the punches. We would talk a lot about our problems, well, I did most of the talking, but we would agree on what we needed to build on. Then the arguments would start again & it was as if we had never spoken at all. As the arguments started to become more frequent, we began to feel like this was normal in a relationship. I would harbour guilt the next day for yelling and she'd feel bad about contributing to the argument, too, yet nothing would get resolved.

By now, I was programmed to deal with confrontation the only way I knew how. I began to feel overwhelmed. My parents weren't impressed. They felt sorry for her, but thought I could do better. I personally thought she was pretty cool, especially with her new fake pink dreadlocks she'd recently had put in.

At the pub that evening, when I went to the toilet and looked in the mirror, I recall talking to myself and feeling there wasn't much about me. I didn't feel handsome at all, so I told myself, "You have done well for yourself...it's not like you can do any better anyway."

Things started to take a turn for the worse. She would

start degrading me in front of my friends, calling me a "lil' bitch" when I insisted we go home earlier than she would have liked. I, in turn, would raise my voice, feeling angry, degraded, and insulted. The arguing became increasingly more toxic. She would raise her voice back at me and I would ramble on and on at her. She made me feel like I had a problem.

It was true that, when I had a problem, even after the heat of the moment, I would go on and on. I wouldn't leave it, but neither would she give my concerns any attention. I, myself, needed resolution. I needed to feel safe and seen. I needed to know that the lesson was learned by both of us, a mistake not to be repeated, as it hurt me so much. For her, it seemed I wouldn't leave the past alone or shut up about it.

Looking back, I'm amazed at how I could keep an argument going. I was able to identify that we both had differing perspectives, but I felt like mine wouldn't be considered. I didn't know at the time that this was from subconscious programming, based on previous arguments with my parents. I had a subconscious belief that said my side would never be heard, and here was my girlfriend, proving my point! You can't find a middle ground without compromise, and she was as unwilling to provide one as my beliefs were unwilling to allow me to see one. As a result, our relationship became one-sided and there was very little comfort.

There was no need to argue. There never is. There is just the best you can do to try and understand where the other person is coming from, or at the very least, have every intention to hold space for. If you cannot hold space at the time, find another time to make them feel heard and cared for. And this is probably the most important thing: make every available opportunity to raise awareness needed around the issues. Don't just kick the dirt under the carpet, so to speak, and leave it unnoticed.

I often rambled for this very reason, I needed space to be heard and cared about. My soul could not grasp the despair, and in turn, I would scream from the rooftops. My ramblings were a desperate cry for help.

My relationship with her became a complete mirror of what was going on at home and in my internal world – all the frustration I was dealing with, how I felt, my beliefs that I wasn't good enough and what I did wasn't good enough. I was told over and over again how my attitude stank, by both her and my parents. I had no template at the time to show me how to focus on the positives or be shown what I could be grateful for. I was well and truly in the victim mentality.

My parents had enough. They told me to get myself

together or to get out. My frustration got the better of me and, feeling unwelcome in my own home, I packed a bag and left, roaming the streets until my mum drove around for an hour, looking down each street for me.

This was not the first time I had threatened to leave home. Each time, I remember feeling devastated, confused, and angry. I felt like I was being bullied for not being acceptable, intentionally punished for being me. I was clearly nothing to my parents, I thought, so I left, upset and misunderstood.

Each time, I would return. Sometimes, no one would answer the door for a little while. Here I was, swanning in and out of my parent's home as I pleased, as if I owned the place, so they might have felt like they had a point to prove. In those moments, while I was waiting, I would see the cat walking through the cat flap into the house and then, moments later, coming back out. I put my head between my legs and cried at the thought that an animal had more freedom and love in my household than I did.

But the only person who was truly denying myself freedom, security, safety, and love (and all those other things you find in a family home) was me. And so, I ran from myself again and into the arms of my girlfriend.

I continued to spiral in this loop, arguing with the girlfriend and then picking up the phone to call my parents for a lift and then ending up back at my girlfriend's house. It didn't matter where I was; I was arguing with everyone. I wasn't good enough and therefore no one else made me feel good enough, either. I was just a shell of myself. But the sex & affection with my girlfriend provided the perfect false sense of security. Until the mask slipped, and we fell back into altercations again.

The final time I left my parents, I packed my car and drove over to her house. They messaged to express their concern, but I had enough evidence that nothing would change between us. My mind was a mess and this loop had caught up with me. I was looking for security and comfort anywhere I could find it, I knew it was no longer available at home.

My girlfriend and I were survivors. Both ungrateful, rarely offering each other compliments, it was no wonder we both had bad attitudes. Everyone involved could see it. Still, we ended up moving into our own place together, away from everyone else. It was just us, facing the world together.

The frustration and anxiety continued to build. Walking back from a night out, one fella smiled at her and said, "Your girlfriend is beautiful. You're lucky to have her." In my intoxicated state, I couldn't recall my reply, but she didn't like it. I tried to comfort her and give her an explanation. Once again, it was lost in translation. We were coming at the argument from two different perspectives. My defensiveness rose and I nudged her on the shoulder, telling her to leave me alone. She lost her momentum and fell.

"Oi! That's no way to treat a woman. Why don't you start on someone your own size? Come and fight a real man, you pathetic piece of shit!" a complete stranger yelled at me, as he approached.

Admittedly, I was intimidated and caught off guard. It had all spiralled out of control and now I had to fight an ignorant-to-the-situation stranger. Luckily, my girlfriend and I managed to defuse the situation, even though we continued arguing the whole way home. If only she and I had been able to cultivate a little empathy & understanding towards each other, it would have made all the difference. It's a shame we didn't know how to.

Perhaps, if I was able to send our younger selves both a letter at the time, it would have read as follows; "Be nice to one another and take the time to listen and understand both perspectives. Retaliating in defence will only escalate the situation, with no opportunity to acknowledge how the other person feels and what is making them think the way they are. What does love mean to each of you? For you must know this, to know if you genuinely love one another.

Otherwise, are you happy to continue the negligence, or worse, trigger each other's insecurities, without learning how to treat yourselves and each other better?"

The truth is, we didn't know how to treat ourselves well, never mind each other. The drinking and drugs didn't help, but what was more damaging was our indoctrinated and insecure behaviour patterns. These just kept re-surfacing and we projected them onto one another. She didn't feel safety or security and neither did I. We were never able to offer one another what we both lacked in ourselves.

On both of us returning home, I wanted to lose myself in that false sense of safety that sex gave me. If we were having sex & giving affection to one another, it was alright. It would balance out the arguments. It wasn't toxic, if we could make up. These were the things I told myself, and I kept my mouth shut to get them.

But this time, as she undressed, she covered up her breasts and kept them covered, as we had sex.

"What are you doing that for? Why are you being insecure? It's such a turn off." I was blunt, brutally so, too honest for my own good.

It was met with a fiery, defensive temper that reignited with force, after the previous arguments of the night. She spat at my face and started putting her hands on me. The most I did in return was to restrain her hands, to stop her blows landing, as she called me a "little bitch" & a "foreign big nosed twat." She knew how to push my buttons, but I had had enough. I put my clothes on and left, walking out and down the street. I thought about calling my parents, when my heart sank. I had left my phone behind. I had no choice but to return, as I had no means to communicate with anyone otherwise.

On my return, she began hurling abuse at me again. I went about, looking for my phone, but couldn't find it, which stirred up more frustration. I got on my hands and knees to look under the bed, when she kicked me. I flipped. Getting up, I pushed her against the wall and, when she spat at me again, I pressed her head away from me into the wall. I really hated her now; she was vile and nasty. Finding my phone, I legged it out of there and went home to my parents.

The next day, the police showed up and I was charged with GBH — Grievous Bodily Harm. I was shocked at the evidence. Her face was bruised here and there; I hadn't realised I had been so rough. It was as if I had used all my might to say physically, "You do not get to hurt me," after she had kicked and spat at me.

The penny dropped when my solicitor said there was a chance of imprisonment. I was just a young man, who had no idea how to express his emotions in a toxic relationship.

Yet, because I was a man who was physically stronger, I was the villain, even though we had both resorted to physical violence.

My solicitor managed to get me to see a parole officer and I was questioned about what happened. After I explained it all and shared about my problems at home with family, which I knew weren't healthy, the parole officer questioned my background. She called it aggressive and called my "foreign morals barbaric." Once again, I was wrong and everyone else was right. This time, though, I was up against the system.

"What do you think about anger management?" the parole officer asked me.

"I don't have anger issues."

"Would you consider doing community service?"

"No, I already work full time. Having to do further work, unpaid, is going to be depressing."

"Well then, it's likely, if you don't go to prison, you'll end up with a suspended sentence."

Which is exactly what I got; an eight-month suspended sentence. That meant, if I got into trouble during those months, I would go straight inside. I felt nothing but relief. I was sorry for the physical pain I had caused my girlfriend and she was sorry, too. We both acknowledged our contribution to the toxic relationship. Perhaps this was it.

Perhaps, we just had to hit rock bottom together, to finally realise what compromise was.

We got another place together, a cosy room in a house-share. I ended up going from job to job, while she was unemployed. A couple of times, we had to shoplift to survive, but it became our new normal. We were survivors and we were happy...until we weren't.

One afternoon, she found my old phone with messages on it, from the start of our relationship three years ago, to another girl.

"What's this? Why the hell were you messaging another girl about going to the cinema, when we were together?"

"Why did you go through my phone? What does it even matter? That happened within days of us getting to know each other. Besides, it's in the past. Nothing happened," I promised her.

"You're disgusting," she bit back. "You might as well have cheated, it's no different. You should feel ashamed of yourself. I'm not going to pay any attention to what you have to say any more."

Well now, that triggered me. Not being seen or heard was that one childhood wound that was always raw. I thought it was so irresponsible and insensitive of her to say that. Whenever I tried to raise my feelings on the matter or explain that my sensitivity was leading me to feel like I couldn't cope, whether with her or my parents, I was told I was "like a woman" or "being silly" – always banging on about my feelings. So, I learned to keep my mouth shut. Without a doubt, it was the reason why I would blow up when I had enough.

I ended up with no choice but to leave the house once again. This time, she followed me.

I asked and begged her to leave me alone, but she wouldn't. She hopped in the car, I requested she get out, all the while screaming at each other. She wouldn't listen to me. I had no space to breathe or think. She continued hurling abuse at me. My frustration built once again to such a point that I grabbed her by the hair and pulled her out of the car. I ran around, locked myself back in the car, but this time, she jumped on the bonnet. I started the engine to call her bluff. She remained on the car. I drove slowly, hoping she would jump off. She didn't. I had no choice but to turn into the car park just up ahead, on my right at a local pub.

When I brought the car to a stop, the police showed up.

What may have helped me to avoid all this trouble was realising that the world and everyone in it was only a reflection of what was going on inside of me.

Most of my problems were self-inflicted by horrible self-talk. I had little respect and admiration for myself. If I had walked and carried myself as if I belonged to this world and shown admiration and respect to all others, I would have had the same courtesy back. Not to say that I didn't at all, I'm just happy to admit that I was ignorant at this point in my life.

There was a quote by Carl Jung about projection that stuck with me. Though I forget it now, here is how I interpreted it. Sometimes, we can feel so certain that we know what another person is like, what they are thinking. But we understand the situation and circumstances they are experiencing from our own point of view and then interact with them based on our own assumptions. What this demonstrates is that perception is not accurate.

My perception at that time in my life was not accurate, and this is why I have come to learn the importance of keeping an open mind and showing courtesy to others. These two things play a huge role in having healthy relationships, not only with others, but with life itself.

With that, I would like you to consider the following. Have you ever stopped for a minute and thought about this? "Every human being, as far as he or she is concerned, is the most important person on earth. You may never get anyone to admit it, but it's a fact." That's a quote from Earl Nightingale's audio tape, A Winner's Attitude. If that quote makes you think, as it made me think, I recommend this exercise, which significantly improved my relationship with others.

For the next thirty days, treat every person you come into contact with, as the most important person on earth, remembering as you do so that, as far as that person is concerned, they are the most important person in their world. What surprised me about treating everyone in this fashion was not only that every human being ought to treat one another like this, but that it also helped me form a habit that brought amazing and delightful results to my life. The same could be true for you, if you give it a try!

We ought to get along with one another, don't you think? After all, frustration has a habit of breeding resentment. Instead, act towards others, and the world at large, in the same manner that you want the world and others to act towards you. Treat your friends, your partner, your family, as the most important people in your life. Then try it with strangers; offer a smile and you might be surprised at how fast you turn into a magnet. That which you seek will begin to naturally gravitate towards you!

Act, walk and talk as the person you wish to become and, almost immediately, you will notice a change in yourself, as I did. Irritations, which used to frustrate and aggravate me, for example, disappeared. Because there is nothing more in this world that we all want and need than to feel like we are important, that we are needed, wanted, and appreciated. We would all give our love and business for the person that will fill this need. The thing we have to realise is, *we* are that person for ourselves.

The trick is to stay on track when someone less informed gives you a hard time. If someone shows you ignorance and lack of courtesy, don't stoop to their level. Leave them to it and do right by yourself.

So, the magic word for this chapter is 'attitude'. If you can form any, it might as well be a good one.

CHAPTER SEVEN:
ARE YOU WORTH IT?

I was arrested with one month remaining on my suspended sentence.

Unfortunately for me, before the court hearing, I felt no need for a solicitor when I gave my statement. I didn't realise when they said, "What you say can and will be used against you in a court of law," it was true. To me, I was in good hands. Surely, I thought, the police could see that I wasn't a bad person.

I needed help and this was the situation at the time.

I had no idea I had signed my sovereignty away, until an hour after my statement had passed. I was locked up in a little cell and, after a while, there was a knock on the door. A little window opened and a voice from the other side of the door spoke.

"Son, why didn't you wait for a solicitor? You've put yourself in a right mess and I can't help you now."

Even when my girlfriend's grandparents prepared a written testament of my character, saying I was a good lad and that my girlfriend and I were going through a bad patch and we were just as bad as each other in our youth and naivety, it didn't work.

The court hearing felt surreal. I was overwhelmed and in handcuffs. The evidence was presented, and my point of view meant nothing. The hearing ruled I was guilty, and I was given six months, three with good behaviour. Everything froze for a minute, and it was as if everything was going by in slow motion. I had no feelings at all; I was absolutely numb, with no other alternative but to meet my fate. I gulped and my heart rate slowed down, with my whole life flashing before my eyes, as the two officers leaned towards me and grabbed hold of the handcuffs. The jury might as well have agreed that I was being sent for execution. It was as if I was being kidnapped. I was helpless. Worse, I felt like I was being treated no different than an animal. I had visions playing out in my mind's eye that I would be stripped to the bare minimum and tortured in the days ahead of me. That's what it felt like, as if I was as good as dead. I was suffering so much on the inside that now I was going to suffer on the outside, too, and the system was going to make sure of it.

I looked at everyone there; no family of my own, only my girlfriend and her grandparents. Their eyes reflected my helplessness back to me. I knew they wanted so badly to help, yet couldn't. Her grandfather was a proud military man and he liked me, so when I could tell he was frightened, I knew it wasn't good. Truth be told, it didn't even cross my mind to tell my own family I was going to court and could potentially face jail time. I knew all too well how disappointed they were, either way. I couldn't bear disappointing them further. Part of me didn't want them to know at all, not to have to break the news. I walked away, ashamed, a disappointment and embarrassment to everyone around me.

My next stop, prison.

I got in the van and off we went. There was no seat. The whole time, I was standing, handcuffed to a bar. I wasn't the only one heading to prison, but I felt alone in that van. Lost, defenceless, hopeless, and withdrawn. As the van drove on, I became more and more numb, just to survive it all.

When we arrived, numbness was replaced with terror. I was terrified for my life. It was like doing the walk of shame to my death sentence. There were metal detectors and scanners to pass through first. Then I had to strip naked. It was requested I do the splits and cough, to ensure nothing was hidden up my bum. Then they checked my mouth cavity and gave me a grey tracksuit with these little white, slip-on shoes, I handed in my belongings, which got bagged up and numbered. After that was sorted, I walked to the office, to talk with the warden.

"I recommend you don't tell anyone why you're here. It

might make you a target among some of the inmates."

I knew being labelled as a woman-beater was frowned upon and, even though that wasn't what had happened, it was the label I was going to get. Now I had to wonder if I was going to get my head kicked in because of it, further confirming that, no matter where I went, I never mattered at all. My life didn't matter, and what I went through didn't matter. My parents were right; I was a piece of shit, no better than an animal in the pecking order now.

Out in the prison jungle, I remained terrified. I kept my head low and spoke only when spoken to. My cheeky self, that had piped up in high school to save my skin, withdrew now I was swimming with the real sharks.

I had thought I was a bit of a bad boy; I knew a few bad boys outside of here and wanted to be like them. Other people treated them cautiously and I wanted to be treated like that, too. So, as I got more comfortable with prison life, I started to come out of my shell and develop a bit of a chip on my shoulder. That was, until the twins showed up.

Everyone treated them with huge respect straight away; everyone knew not to mess with them. I was surprised, until I discovered they had been in and out of this prison more times than I could count. They didn't give two fucks about anything. They had smuggled in enough heroin to keep them going for the length of their sentence. Others had smuggled in phones - I was amazed what fitted inside the body - but heroin was something else. I was nothing, compared to these two. I wasn't a bad boy. I wasn't one of these people that just wanted to watch the world burn.

Luckily for me, I came across a good bunch of people in there, who had my back. Some were right hard nuts, proper tough lads with no fear or any insecurities, as far as I could see. My roommate was one of them. One night, he asked me to turn the light off and I told him to do it himself. He came up beside me, clenching his fists, gritting his teeth, as if he wanted to give me a good kicking, but I remained calm and just left him to it. Tensions eased and I got up to turn the light off.

When I moved cells, my new roommates were smoking heroin, and one of them asked me how I would feel if I woke up with a condom hanging out of my arse. Luckily for me, they were joking. After a while of pretending to sleep with one eye open, I let the fear subside and fell asleep just fine. All those years, building a chip on my shoulder, putting my guard up, trying to stand up to the bullies and the "alpha males" in school had finally taught me my lesson...throwing attitude at others got you nowhere.

And so, the days in prison ticked along. My girlfriend's nan was nice enough to send me money for my canteen, once a week. One week, the payment didn't come through and I was out of tobacco, so I borrowed it off one of the lads I had heard was alright. He only requested "double bubble", meaning I had to pay back double what I owed, but otherwise he was pretty easy-going.

A week passed and still there was no money in my canteen account. It turns out my girlfriend's nan had entered one of the digits wrong and the money had been sent over to another prisoner. A paedophile, the guards told me, when I went to investigate.

"Is there anything I can do about it?" I asked.

"No," the guard replied.

I had no choice but to ask the guy I had borrowed fags from for more time. He wasn't patient. He came and threatened me in my cell. If I didn't get him his fags, I was fucked, he told me, as he held what looked like a kitchen knife in his trousers. There was no mistaking what he meant. That day, I realised my life was valuable to me and I carved out a knife, made from a pen and a shaver, using a lighter to fuse the two. I was aware of the danger of being caught with a homemade blade, but I had finally learnt my most important lesson to date. My life mattered.

You might remember that, earlier, I spoke about the hierarchy of the status quo, the jungle I compared it to. Well, prison most certainly upped the stakes for me. I could see the different attitudes of the men, the same way I saw the different characteristics of animals. The jackal, for example, was swift about his terrain, making quick estimations to survive. This, however, made him judgemental. The hedgehog protected himself, but wasn't kind to himself. He was rather fragile and defensive. The meerkat was observational, evaluating before taking any action, leading to being lost in his own mind, overthinking. The whale was self-aware, intuitive, and empathetic. Of all the mammals, though, the one I found most fascinating was the giraffe. With his long neck, he gained the greatest clarity of all the others in the animal kingdom. For me, if I could be any of these animals, I would most definitely choose to be the giraffe. I would have a better perspective and be better be able to observe from a big open-hearted space.

Although all these traits serve their purpose, in prison, I most definitely had to adapt from one to another to survive. Some of these traits can be pretty toxic in comparison to others and do impact the quality of your life, whichever jungle you find yourself in. It is my hope that, just as I gained better clarity by wondering which animal trait I was choosing at any given moment, you can also.

What does it mean to breathe and fight, to live for another day in the animal kingdom? My experience in prison is far from a healthy analogy.

Yes, my life matters and that same truth applies to you!

Many of us don't realise the damage our old habits do, the stories we tell ourselves and our negative thinking that we continue to inflict upon ourselves, day in, day out.

The thoughts we think, the words we speak, and the actions we take constantly shape our world & experiences. Thankfully, none of this is fixed and we can make a change. How so? By first of all, being aware that you do have a choice & that you can consistently choose positive thoughts about what matters to you. With that, the old negative thoughts we tell ourselves will start to dissolve away.

So, let's focus on the main problem; our limiting beliefs.

Speaking for myself, I have made countless mistakes over the years. This shaped my mind to always think two steps ahead (negatively, unfortunately, which did not help).

Do you recall when I described the nervous system in chapter one? Well, this is not only made up of the fight or flight mode, but it's also responsible for our primitive survival coping mechanisms. Once upon a time, when we were primitive humans, we had to navigate our terrain and be aware of lions, for example, so we trod carefully and roamed in survival mode, hence the two steps ahead mechanism. This aspect still remains with us, to this day.

What does that have to do with our limiting beliefs? Well, you no longer have to be aware of lions, but your nervous system still feels the need to protect you. That's what your limiting beliefs THINK they are doing. It's fair to say, you've probably been listening to these pesky limiting beliefs unknowingly. Without any conscious awareness, you have likely been stopping yourself from crossing the finish line, before you've even started the race. You might have, perhaps without knowing, become obsessed and distracted by making excuses and convincing yourself that you can't do something. Meanwhile, you haven't given yourself the opportunity to even try, because you've been listening to those limiting beliefs in your head.

Here is the thing, though, even if you did try, you might have failed. And this would have reinforced that limiting belief, making you even MORE likely to give up.

This reminds me of a story by Thomas Edison, who invented the light bulb. Did you know that it took him one thousand attempts, before he succeeded? Did you know that his assistant insisted he stop? To which he replied, "Every time I fail, I'm closer to how not to make the same mistake and thus succeeding." Now, imagine if he hadn't bothered, if he'd lost hope and given up at the five hundredth attempt.

Are you prepared to give yourself the same chance with your own life? I could have listened to my limiting beliefs and let them stop me writing this book, scared of what others (including my family) might have thought about me. I could have listened to the limiting belief that being this vulnerable was something to be scared of (it is, to this day, my biggest fear). Instead, I chose to ignore them and do it anyway.

How was I able to do so? By realising it wasn't about me or my beliefs at all. In my own way, I was contributing towards humanity and living with purpose. The best part about all of this has been that I'm doing something I really enjoy and am passionate about sharing. When I can focus on these positives, the negative limiting beliefs begin to dissolve away. Because, trust me, if I had listened to them, I would have made out like an ostrich and buried my head in the sand! I likely would have taken these words to my deathbed.

Limiting beliefs can completely destroy your goals and diminish your quality of life, if you let them. So, here are a few steps for identifying and overcoming your limiting beliefs.

Step 1 – Identify them

Ask yourself, if you had all the time and money in the world, what would you do? What is actually stopping you? Get to the root cause and be really honest with yourself.

Don't make excuses about time or money. What is the belief behind the excuse that is stopping you?

I'll share with you one of my own examples. If I had all the money and time in the world, I would take every opportunity to inspire others to make the most out of their own lives. This would make me feel like I was of service and contributing towards a fulfilling life (not only for myself, but my family and society as a whole).

What are my limiting beliefs, stopping me from doing this some days? Well, I think...I am no one special, I have a lot of work on my own self to do, I need to walk the walk and not only give it the *billy big bollocks*. I also think, what is everyone going to think of me? And does anyone actually care about me? (This is a big limiting belief that will come up as you hear more of my story.)

As you can see, from my example, once you ask this question, you can come to understand your limiting beliefs. You'll be able to see with your own emotional and intellectual intelligence, why you are getting the results you are getting, rather than the results you desire. But that also means you can understand how to change that and live a better quality of life!

Step 2 – Develop confidence

The more focused you are about something, the more attention you are giving it. What are the limiting beliefs you have addressed and what are the polar opposites of them? How does it make you feel? Can you begin to imagine what it might look like, living to your full potential?

Let's look at my limiting beliefs again, as an example. First of all, I came to understand that "special" is a matter of attitude and where I dare decide to place my attention. So, as for the belief that I am no one special, the obvious conclusion in polarity to that is that I am special. Of course, I deserve to feel like that is the case! And why not? If you had children, wouldn't you want them to feel special?

Practice telling yourself the polarity of your limiting beliefs, day in and day out, for as long as you can. Write it out a hundred times, as descriptively as you can, and enact it, as if it is real. Recall what I said earlier about the subconscious mind not knowing the difference between imagination and reality and that, if you can have any attitude, you might as well make it a good one. Anything you dwell on grows in your reality, so plant positive seeds that harbour the fruit of your desired labour.

Step 3 – Build clarity and take action

Take a piece of paper and write down twelve goals that you would like to accomplish in the next twelve months. Now, imagine waving a magical wand over the list, knowing that you are able to accomplish one of these goals within the next twenty-four hours, which will yield you the best results in your life. Whichever goal comes to mind is the one you want to prioritise. That becomes your purpose from now on. Give yourself a deadline as to when you would like to accomplish it and list all the things you need to do, in order to achieve it.

Again, let's look at one of my own examples. I took every opportunity to invest into my own self, taking part in programmes or hiring coaches. I might not have been able to technically afford them and fall back on the limiting belief that "I can't afford it and how will I pay for this?" But, unless I gave myself the chance and made up my own mind that I would do it, every excuse under the sun would have come up instead. It would have stopped me from creating the circumstances to make everything I've said possible. With the help of these coaches, I looked at my phone for the first time and saw the potential to engage with so many people worldwide. I now use social media to raise awareness about my own interests and views, through live videos, and am building a community, by joining key groups related to my core values. As time went on, I realised I was investing in myself, by acting through whatever means necessary.

Step 4 – Commit with consistency

When you identify what is holding you back, create an unshakable confidence that you can do anything you want, and then make a plan for exactly how to do it. You will become free of limiting beliefs and be on your way to becoming unstoppable, towards a better-quality way of life.

Social media offered me the opportunity to put myself out there and confront my fears, by getting comfortable with feeling vulnerable. I would not have otherwise been able to write this book, unless I shamelessly hid behind it anonymously.

It took commitment, it took courage, but if – like me – you decide to take on these four steps every day, you're one step away from reprogramming your self-image and becoming the person you naturally want to engage with the world as. Remember, there are no limits on what you can achieve with your life, except the limits you place on your own mind.

CHAPTER EIGHT: BACK OUT IN THE REAL WORLD

The day I got out of prison, my friends came to pick me up. What could they even say?

I wasn't proud of the circumstances that I had been living in these last few months, so I just smiled and carried on as normal, as best I could. But even they could see I wasn't at my best. I had lost a stone and looked really pale. I had shaved my head in prison, too; it was easier to maintain and looked more presentable. It emphasised how I felt inside, mind you – withdrawn. I wasn't the Antonio they knew anymore.

They dropped me off at my girlfriend's, where she was waiting for me, and we spent a passionate night, reunited. I put off seeing my parents for as long as possible. I knew all too well of the disappointment I would receive. Sure enough, when the time came around, they felt sorry for me. I didn't look too well and what a hard sight for my parents that must have been to see.

They expressed their thoughts on my life so far and questioned my relationship. They asked if I had learnt my lesson. This, however, turned into an argument. Life out of prison was just like before. Nothing had changed. I ran back to my girlfriend and did what I always did; I smoked weed. Except, this time, I didn't have a job. I was smoking weed, playing video games, & making instrumental beats.

I loved getting high and creating music; I felt like I was in my element. The truth of it was, I was lost in the moment when I was with my imagination, and it felt like I was doing something purposeful when I was creating. Now, knowing what I know about what it means to be human, I can see the irony in what I was doing.

Steve Bow probably says it better: "God's gift to you is more talent and ability than you will use in one lifetime. Your gift to God is to develop and utilise as much of that talent and ability as you can in this lifetime."

How beautiful.

I did my best to look for work, but in all honesty, I felt hopeless. I lived from the back pocket of my girlfriend and whatever financial aid I could get from the government. I had been institutionalised. To escape that fact, to escape from myself and my life, I monged out on weed. The old Antonio had been social, but from here on out, I kept myself to myself and hardly left the house. I was a recluse.

One day, while my girlfriend was at work, I went downstairs. I noticed one of the lads from our house-share, passed out in the lounge, sleeping. On the dining room table was a fair amount of weed. I'd run out, so I helped myself. How sad and desperate I was that I resorted to stealing from someone I shared a roof with. It wasn't the first thing I'd helped myself to; I'd also gone into his room and helped myself to hair clippers. (Come to think of it, I didn't ever hand them back.)

I don't know whether he woke up and saw me take it through a squinted eye or just assumed it was me. After all, I had a reputation in the house, since all I did was smoke in my room and have the volume up loud, whilst playing video games or making music. But one night, the lodgers weren't having it anymore.

One of them had her boyfriend over and, after a few drinks, she began to express her annoyance at me and my behaviour, not that I knew it, until her fella burst into our room one evening. He was covered in tattoos and obviously fancied himself a tough guy. He probably wanted to show his girlfriend how tough he was. With all due respect, I was a stranger in the house, who had stolen stuff from another lodger and was a liability. He had every right to confront and challenge me.

I should have known better. In prison, I learned that stealing would have cost you your life, and those guys were much tougher than this one. Did my freedom mean I could now do whatever I wanted? Is that what I believed? What a mess I was.

As he knelt down close to my face, I could see a studded belt wrapped around his wrist. He was shouting and threatening to kick my head in. Both my girlfriend and I were shocked and scared. He'd just barged in and started going off on one! Then it dawned on me why this must be the case...the weed I had helped myself to the other day.

I played out the scenario in the back of my mind, while he was yelling at me. I thought of the staircase on the landing. If I was to get up and go for him, I thought, chances were that we would head right into the landing and this fella and I would end up tumbling down the stairs. I eyed up the ceramic ashtray...but I was worried if I went for his head, it might possibly look like murder. I was fresh out of prison, and any more trouble would warrant me heading right back in!

I was in despair; I didn't know what to do and none of the scenarios looked good. So, I played into his hands how sorry I was. He soon left the room, feeling sorry for me. I hadn't given him any attitude, for one; I had learnt that lesson in prison. Or perhaps he anticipated the scenarios I had played out in my mind, too. Maybe he had seen me eyeing up the ceramic ashtray. Either way, he would have felt my fear, and that must have brought him some comfort - enough to back off and leave me be.

That night was our cue to leave, though. We weren't

welcome anymore, so we packed up what we could right away and ended up leaving for my parents'. The cycle had repeated once more. This time, though, it was nice. My mum and dad made every effort to make us feel welcome and looked after us. We weren't there long before we found a property to move into together and shortly left.

It was a nice, little flat. We had a good time, threw parties, and enjoyed ourselves, although we still argued a lot. My girlfriend would return home to find out I'd masturbated while she was gone. For her, it was as if I had cheated on her. For me, it was simply meeting a sexual need, but she must have linked her self-worth to her sexuality and my actions triggered her. When I looked for a different release in masturbation, I must have minimised her worth, in her mind. I couldn't see reason in her logic, and she couldn't see reason in mine. She was not to know how desperately unhappy or depressed I was, even though I was out of prison.

So, the arguments began to escalate again. In the end, we would have huge bust-ups about the most mundane things. One day, I had become fed up that she never prepared food or made arrangements, so I asked her to help with dinner. When she went to help me, I expressed how her laziness bothered me and she lost her mind, throwing a kitchen knife at me. After all, who was I to talk?

I was jobless most of the time, living out of her back pocket.

The cycle continued. I got stuck in a loop of being in and out of jobs, arguing with my girlfriend and ending up in and out of my parents'. After being back with my parents for a while, I found out she had cheated on me with her boss. My hunch was that he had been there hours before I returned. But eventually, as per the inevitable loop, I ended up getting back with her.

This time, she had found a bigger place on her own. I felt guilty for arguing, like I was to blame and had to fix things. She felt sorry for me, so we decided to give it another go. Except, while she was away on holiday, I tried to get my revenge and sleep with another woman. When she returned, her intuition told her to check my laptop. She found all the evidence. Surprisingly, this time she was calm. Maybe because nothing had physically happened. Maybe because she had seen it coming. Maybe because she thought she deserved it, after her betrayal before. It had even crossed my mind to wonder if she had been unfaithful while she was away on holiday, and I was on my own before she returned. It's plausible that maybe she was just as sick of us arguing as I was. So that night, out of guilt, I asked her if we should have a child, to right our wrongs. We had passionate sex with one another, smiling at the thought of being parents in the next coming few months.

As time went on, nothing changed between us. We still ended up fighting with each other. One night, I left out the kitchen window, terrified the police would be outside, as we screamed abuse at each other.

When she fell pregnant, it changed something in me. We had moved back into my parents' as a means of support, while we tried to get a property from the council. In the meantime, I found a job I was content with. I became a plasterer's labourer. I admired the fact that he always had loads of cash; I wanted that for myself and my family. I found my purpose, my mission for my son. It wasn't easy, as the boss was as mad as a box of frogs, but I put my head down, worked hard and was able to make a respectable wage.

But it wasn't to be. While we were in a midway home by ourselves, waiting to be housed by the council, we fell back into old habits and argued heavily. Except, this time, I couldn't put up with the swearing anymore, not in front of my one-year-old son. So, I left.

I hadn't realised leaving also meant leaving my son behind, full-time. I missed him, my parents couldn't comfort me, and the mother of my child got involved with another man. Months passed and my depression deepened.

One day, we were both at her nan's. I was there to see

my son, but she was unaware I was there, until she arrived. The moment she walked into the room and saw me, she fell to her knees, apologised for everything and begged for us to get back together. Deep in depression with no boundaries, I agreed.

We got back together again, but the time apart still hadn't changed our patterns. In fact, it made things worse. One day, she laughed about how she used to have a go at me for masturbating. "Oh, the guy I dated after you made me realise it's normal. He used to masturbate all the time, too! I realised how silly I was to think of it as cheating."

She had probably meant it as a way to reassure me of her changed ways, but all I felt was insulted. Like this other guy had been *allowed* to be himself and I hadn't. There it was again, my ugly insecurities coming up. In all honesty, it hurt like hell.

Eventually, I realised I couldn't let go of the past, although I knew all too well our instinctive patterns. We both have to change, and we couldn't do it together. You might say that I finally broke the toxic loop. This time, however, there was no escaping us. We had a child together.

It's funny how we seem to live under the illusion that we can fix things quickly, particularly in relationships. It takes a lot of work; it takes talking to one another often and compromising. But most of us want it fixed right now. When I realised this (much later in my life, after the breakdown of my relationships), I began to see how life is indeed short and that we waste it by having little belief in our own power to just rise up, have faith, courage and determination to withstand the wind and walk on.

With that, I would like to add, where trust issues are concerned with others, you might want to consider seeking professional help from a relationship counsellor. It's ok to want to seek out and ask for help. This will help you develop a healthy setting, where you can both feel supported and encouraged, as you get vulnerable and transparent with each other. I speak from experience. Most of us usually turn to family and friends for relationship advice, but they often come with their own biases. A professional offers neutral ground.

I would also strongly urge you to self-inquire, write out the pros and cons of the relationship, establish your own boundaries and do right by yourself and each other. Minimise any collateral damage, but do not jeopardise your future. Most importantly, respect yourself!

It won't always be easy addressing these things in your relationships with others. You have to be ok with sometimes feeling like shit, to just cry and feel the feels. But always make space afterwards to put things into perspective. Don't ignore the circumstances and kick the dirt under the carpet; address it. And, most importantly, have courtesy for one another.

One of the best ways to improve any relationship, especially the one with yourself, is to start to get thankful. This exercise helped me a lot in moving forward from a relationship, to realise that I could go with the motions and, at the same time, rise to be better for my family.

Here it is.

I would like you to get out a piece of paper and write down your age and make an estimate as to how many years you might have left to live.

I'll start with myself. As it stands, I am thirty-five. I would say I have at least another fifty years, give or take, yet to live. Now, let's say I see my parents once a month; by calculation, I will get to see them six hundred times in my lifetime.

Why do I share this with you? I want to help you begin to look at your life from another perspective. What else do you get to do? Who do you get to see that means the world to you? On the flip side, what are you doing that your future self can thank you for later?

Now, let's look at my estimate for how long I think I have left to live; fifty years, right? Let's look at it another way. What if we look at it as only having fifty summers left to enjoy? That's a whole new perspective! In terms of years, it sure seems like a long time, but in terms of how many summers, it doesn't seem as much! How many of us take for granted how precious our time is? We spend most of our time wishing our lives away, living for the weekend, wishing away the winter, so that we may enjoy ourselves when summer comes along. Worse still, holding on to the past and not making way for other opportunities that could, without a doubt, be auspicious, if you allow them and believe in yourself!

It is with this simple change of perspective that I hope to remind you to appreciate the little things in life. To appreciate what you have right now, for you may not otherwise be able to appreciate what is yet to come. When you think about it, tomorrow never comes. All there ever is, is right now.

There will be days when you find yourself feeling blue. There will be days when you find yourself tired. There will be days when you feel overwhelmed. What I want you to know is that it is ok. It's fine to feel all these emotions surfacing. Just as the weather goes through cycles, so do we.

Remember what I said about limiting beliefs? One thing we also seem to do is make out like everything has to be perfect all the time. You have to be ok with wanting to take time out, for feeling whatever is going on. But never forget how many summers you have to come, and at every opportunity, make the most of what is. Do the best with what you've got and make something magnificent with what you have, whatever that may be for you. Enjoy the snowball fights, embrace the storms, snuggle up and enjoy the cold, light up a candle or two when it's dark.

Most importantly, cherish your awareness. There are no quick fixes. Things take time. Even with all that might seem to be going wrong in your world, it has the potential to teach you a lesson or two. Always be taking a step forward and be ok with taking a step or two back, but have certainty that taking ANY step is better than not taking any steps at all. One day, you will find yourself taking one monumental step, and then find yourself skipping and whistling in all weathers, no matter the circumstances, taking every opportunity you have to make the most of your life.

CHAPTER NINE:
ROCK BOTTOM

It was not easy being a single dad, living back home with my parents. I had lost everything, including my son. Sure, I got to see him once in a while. But it wasn't the same as having been with him every day.

I was in bits, heartbroken. His mother would come over to drop him off in the Toyota Celica that I had signed over to her name, as an indication of how much I valued her. It had been the nicest car we had to date and was the nicest thing I could do for her at the time. And she would be all dressed up, as if she was going out on a date. It killed me. I broke down into a million pieces once she left, and while I should have been grateful that I would get to spend time with my son, I just couldn't quite function. Absorbed in the pain, all I wanted to do was cry. I couldn't give my son the attention he needed from me.

The relationship between her and me became that of hate for one another. I resented her for all the damage she had contributed towards us and her lack of empathy for me. She resented me for always bringing up issues. She hated that! No matter how I expressed myself, I felt I couldn't talk from my perspective. It was as if I was talking to a brick wall and all I kept hearing was "that I go on and on and won't leave it alone." I just needed her to care, but to me, her response and actions proved otherwise. Once again, my insecurities came to the surface; to feel that I didn't matter and what I said was out of line. My frustration and anger at not being seen or heard, my desire for understanding and expressing, were somehow against me.

I now understand why. The harsh reality is that everyone has their own perspective and is free to think what they like. Talking will most likely not change their mind, as most of the time, their mind has been made up. You might believe yourself to be right, as will they, and so it might hurt to realise someone you love won't see eye to eye with you. But what I came to learn matters most is: not to seek validation, but to be independent with a positive attitude, good intentions, and compassion for yourself, as well as them. If you can approach a relationship like this, you don't feel like you are battling to be heard! Your actions will speak for themselves.

Back then, some weeks, I didn't see my son at all. In her mind, she must have felt like I had crossed the line with how I was talking to her. Admittedly, I was projecting how I felt, I was upset and in a lot of pain.

"You're not only punishing me," I'd tell her.

I would think to myself that, out of a year, as it stood at the time, I would only see my son for around fifty-two days. My dad wasn't around much when I was younger, and I didn't want the same for my own child. Never mind having thoughts that, when my son's mother moved on, another man would be around him more than I could wish for.

I felt like a bad parent, too, which was only amplified by my arguments with my parents about my decision-making. By now, I was losing everyone, as my friends had no time for me, either. I had nothing to offer anyone. I had no job, no money, I was depressed, with low self-esteem, and so I turned into an energy vampire and scrounger to anyone who approached me. I was only existing, a shell of myself. I had little patience for my son, given how self-absorbed I was, despite wanting to see him desperately. I was so focused on how worthless and empty I felt, I was unable to be present.

One day, a former boss of mine invited me down to the seaside to party with his friends. What did I have to lose? It sounded like a promising night. My boss was a laugh, and his friends, from what I had heard, were alright, as well. A boys' night out to town; this was just what I needed. To make it really fun, we decided to score some cocaine. But having left it to the last minute, we weren't having any luck.

"I'll make a few phone calls," I said.

On one of those phone calls, the dealer said they had some Mkat.

"Mkat, what is that?" I asked.

"Mate, this stuff will blow your head off."

"What's it like, then?"

"Like cocaine and MDMA combined. Trust me mate, you will love it."

Mkat is a type of methamphetamine that, believe it or not, was introduced into local shops, legally. To get away with it, there was a loophole. It was sold under "plant fertiliser", as a means to discredit the real agenda for it, even though it had a label on it saying, "Not for human consumption."

Yeah, right.

It was mainly sold in music shops; in particular, the places where you went to purchase concert tickets. So many of us got addicted to it. It was dead cheap and most of us consumed it throughout the day, each and every day.

For me, I developed my own love affair with it, which started on that boys' night out.

I said I would get back to the dealer and called my former boss, who said, "Yeah, fuck it." To our surprise, it was one tenth of the price, compared to cocaine, so we all agreed to take advantage and get a few. Seeing as I organised the deal, I drove over to the dealer to pick it up. Once I had it, I decided to make a stop and do a line of it. Sure enough, just like matey said, it blew my mind.

Cranking the music up, I drove away, exhilarated. I was pumped and raring to go! I pulled into the carpark.

"Boss, I'm outside waiting for you. Wait until you try this stuff I got us; it's amazing!"

On the way to town, I scared the living daylights out of him, driving like a right nutter. I had the music up really loud, and we were chewing each other's ears off, cracking up at jokes. But, in the state that I was in, one false move and it would have been goodnight - or worse. Luckily, we made it to the location safely and had a really good laugh that night. I had no luck with the ladies, mind you; my insecurity and paranoia were enough to put any girl off.

Not that it mattered, because I had a new relationship in my life. Mkat became a substance I could use to enjoy and escape my reality with. I would find myself lost in the moment with it. I felt like, whatever I was dealing with emotionally, and whatever thoughts usually crowded my mind, disappeared. I felt relieved.

The next weekend, I was due to have my son over the weekend, but his mother and I ended up in another one of our arguments. When she hung up the phone telling me to, "Fuck off, you're not seeing your son now," I was in bits again.

What else could I do, apart from be depressed and most likely end up texting her all night, arguing?

"Fuck it," I thought, and I decided to pick up the phone and call the dealer.

I picked up a gram later that night and headed off home. It was late in the evening by now and everyone was in bed. So, I had a line here and there and was listening to music, when I decided to enjoy myself and have a wank. I went to masturbate and here is where the penny dropped. My jaw hit the floor in disbelief. On Mkat, it was as if every stroke of my penis was an orgasm. The sensation felt incredible. I couldn't get enough.

How could this be? I wondered. I went from one stroke to another, engulfed by pleasure.

Looking back now, I had no idea what I was getting myself into. It was as if I was wearing rose-tinted glasses. It was almost too good to be true and so it was! But I was in complete denial.

One thing led to another and, instead of just getting one gram, I would now get two. Something that would last me a couple of hours or so before, would now last me throughout the night. I would take the opportunity to snort it later on in the day, whenever everyone went off to bed (I was living with my parents at the time, where my sister and brother also lived). When I noticed everyone had locked themselves away in their own bedrooms, I would proceed with excitement to masturbate.

One evening, I was so aroused, I couldn't take it. I had snorted one massive line in each nostril and the euphoria was overwhelming, almost too much. It was so intense that I could feel myself pre-cumming, & I wasn't even touching myself. I began to play with myself, and I started to feel different parts of my anatomy that I'd never felt before. As I began to start to touch myself, it felt like the most natural urge to want to reach for my perineum. It felt as though it was pulsating, which led me to move towards my bumhole. My heart rate skyrocketed as I inserted a finger. I let out a loud sigh that made me bite my tongue to quiet myself. It made touching my penis so much more intense!

The comedown, however, was awful.

I would be horrified with what I had been up to. I might have managed to then sleep for an hour or two, but given that I was sleeping in the lounge, I would be woken up by my mum walking in, trying to get access to the garden and asking what the smell was. It was from the chemicals I had been snorting for most of the night.

"No idea," I exclaimed.

I just wanted to bury my head and die, seeing her face, looking at me with disgust. Curling up thereafter into a ball, withdrawing, I became a shadow of myself.

My dad even walked in on me one night. Luckily for me, he walked in a minute later or he would have seen me up to all sorts with myself, lying there naked, a sweaty mess on the sofa bed. Nothing was said as he turned around and walked back out, closing the door. Once or twice, in the morning, I would rush into the kitchen to attempt to explain myself and admit I had a problem and ask for help.

My mum would look at me as if to say, "Go on then. I know what you've been up to, shame yourself."

In her glare, I saw mockery and disgust. It was almost like she was baiting me into confessing what she already knew.

And so, with that, I shrivelled and muttered, "Never mind," as I walked away.

"Leave him," I would hear my dad say.

And so, I was left to chase the high of Mkat and explore my newfound curiosity, to find out what was in my bum that gave me such pleasure. I researched on the internet and discovered that, when you are in your mother's womb, right before the chromosomes form & dictate what gender you become, just as a woman has a g-spot, a man still keeps that part of the anatomy, although it forms in what is known as the prostate. Stimulation of the prostate could induce a body-quivering, multiple orgasm, like a woman with the g-spot!

Now this I had to experience! It sounded remarkable. What I had experienced so far felt so good; how could it possibly get better?

I was yet to have an orgasm or ejaculate while under the influence of Mkat. When I was sober, I would find myself fantasising about the next opportunity, although by now, I was starting to question my sexuality.

I was led to believe you had to be gay to discover that side of your anatomy. But it was only when I was under the influence of Mkat that I would indulge in that sort of activity. I never felt comfortable doing that when I was sober; that wasn't for me to explore, unless I was high. It just seemed like the only logical thing to do at the time, considering the euphoria and as a consequence of having very little to no inhibitions when I indulged in Mkat. In the morning, whenever I explored this aspect of myself after a session with Mkat, the thought of what I had been up to for most of the night made me feel uncomfortable. I judged myself harshly and felt terribly ashamed.

I had to be as kind to myself as much as possible, as hard as that was, while I was having panic attacks and that horrible sinking feeling in my chest. The feeling that what I was doing was wrong, the sleaziness of it all, the act of being off my head, going from one porno to the next, with my dick in my hand, and the comedown afterwards, drove my dopamine levels down, as I went deeper into depression. The thought that I brought attention to myself in my family home also only brought on more guilt and shame. For days afterwards, I would wallow, feeling nauseous. I felt so lost and didn't care if I lived or died, to be honest.

Mkat offered no inhibitions, and my mind - desperate to no longer feel the pain of the trauma I'd experienced in life - sought out the relief and pleasure the drugs gave me. It became the only habit I had to look forward to, with nothing else to live for.

One day, when my sister confronted me about it, I got defensive and told her to fuck off. She came from a place of judgement, and I didn't feel much care was being directed at me.

"You don't know how I feel," I yelled. "I can't bear it, I'm suffering, and I'm depressed. I don't know how to live, and I feel like I'd be better off dead. What do you know about that?"

Confrontation, it turned out, wasn't what I needed. It was compassion and understanding. The arguments I was having with everyone; my ex, my parents, my friends, my sister, did nothing to help. The toxicity of the relationships I was in led me to cower away under the rock I climbed up from every night, before I knew better. Night after night, I returned to the substances that masked my own feelings and the thoughts that consumed me, by returning to pleasure.

Let's look at what it means to hit rock bottom. It's a horrible place and I speak from experience, having felt the feelings of guilt, shame, and embarrassment. Looking back to all the times when I didn't care whether I lived or died, how did I lift myself back up and how did I begin to have a transformational shift?

By coming to understand the following three steps.

Step 1 – Ask yourself, what is the point of wallowing in the feeling of guilt, shame, and embarrassment? Is living with regret serving you? Would you be happy to remain feeling like this, five years from now? If not, what are you going to do about it? This opens the spectrum of what you are giving your life to. So, moving forward, how can you begin to heal?

Step 2 – Take any opportunity you can to have a heart to heart with yourself. Bear this in mind as you do; you are responsible for your life and you are responsible for your own feelings. You are responsible for your own personal growth, and you are responsible for every result you get.

Hold yourself fully accountable, without blame, and own your story! From there, a gold mine will unravel, with insight to so many lessons. I, for example, never realised I hated myself. But once I had that revelation in my heart to heart, I realised I needed to get the lockdown on self-love. From there, my personal development grew, which in turn, helped me ignite some new passions for life!

Step 3 – Write out a hundred things you love about yourself. Take all the time in the world and get to know every aspect about yourself, which is worth loving. You might have taken some of these traits for granted, you might have not thought about it and might not have otherwise placed any attention on them. We have a habit of measuring ourselves, based on the validations of others. I say it's time to start realising all the lovable aspects of yourself and for you to start recognising how wonderful you are. Now, I'll be honest, it took a great deal of effort for me to even write ten at first, never mind a hundred. But you will surprise yourself, if you pay no attention to the time it takes and allow nothing to distract you. Put a smile on your face and embrace the process with an open heart, determined to find out all the loveable aspects of yourself. It will make a remarkable change from a lifetime of picking out your flaws; trust me.

CHAPTER TEN: SEX ADDICTION & LOVE

By this time, I was starting to become aware that I was bringing unwanted attention to myself. I found comfort in the idea of going out to "play", late in the evening, parked up somewhere private.

This time round, I went to a sex shop. It felt like the next stage, as I found myself curious about sex toys, so off I went. I couldn't believe what I saw there. I was a nervous wreck, although the idea of what I was going to get up to that night was arousing, as I looked at all the content on the shelves. I grabbed a few toys and went to pay. On the top shelf, behind the counter, I noticed a few bottles. I asked the assistant what they were.

"Those are Poppers," he said.

"Poppers?"

"Yeah, they're great. You open the lid and snort the vape. It heightens your senses and loosens up all your muscles."

Fuck it, that sounds like it will go hand in hand with what I have planned, I thought to myself.

I even took out the packets of Mkat I had in my pocket and showed him what I had. I stunned him; he stumbled back a bit at my openness. Then he leaned forward, smiled, and gave me a wink.

Driving off grid as best I could, I found a quiet spot to park up, with no houses nearby and no streetlights either. This spot looked perfect. I stopped and proceeded to empty the contents of the bag from the sex shop. I racked up a few massive lines of Mkat, snorted two or three of them, then twisted the lid off the Poppers.

I didn't know what planet I was on after that. From that moment on, I was engulfed by sensations far exceeding what I had previously grown accustomed to. I spent hours lost in the moment, masturbating, and moaning my lungs out. Hours later, however, I started to get paranoid.

I spent many evenings like this, ending the night on a wild goose chase, driving from one location to the next, thinking that people were after me. Even in the heat of the moment, I was like a meerkat, keeping an eye out for any cars or walkers nearby.

And still, I wanted to experience this over and over again, on drugs. I hadn't achieved an orgasm as of yet, never mind the experiences I had read about online, and so that was my intention, every time I turned to the drugs. It grew to be the only thing I looked forward to.

I spent countless hours on the internet, looking up other people's experiences, with an apprehensive beating heart for my next opportunity to try and achieve it.

I thought meeting a woman might be the way to go about it, in the comfort of company. But I was off my head on drugs and so many of the women I met were, too – the way the Universe always mirrors yourself back to you. I was never comfortable around them. One way or another, my only intention never made it to fruition, which became very frustrating. Namely, because I was uncomfortable opening up and asking for what I really wanted, although we would talk about it by text. In person, however, I wasn't comfortable with myself, and neither were they, as a result.

Then, one day, I met a lovely woman. We met online and planned to meet at the last minute in person, when we got to talking, as I had the day off, and so did she, and her son was at school. She invited me over for a cup of tea. She was welcoming and warm, & we had a great time, enjoying each other's company.

One evening, I went round to hers with a cheeky thought in my mind and grabbed a few grams of Mkat to store in my pocket. As the night went on, I pulled it out and asked if she would indulge me. She joined me and did a few lines, too. Would you believe it, she didn't hesitate and actually joined me! Wow, did we have a great time! One thing led to another and we had a wonderful night.

Kissing her was unlike anything I'd experienced before.

The touch of her lips pressed onto mine felt magical, like it was meant to be. That's the only way I can describe it. It was perfect.

I ran out the house at one point, quick off my feet, to the van, to grab the bag of toys I'd hidden under my passenger seat. Running back, I closed the door and emptied the bag in front of her. You should have seen her face! It's fair to say she probably thought I was going to use them on her, and I did. Although, I stunned her when I suggested she use them on me, as well. In the heat of the moment, she went for it.

It must have seemed like a good idea at the time, but I could tell she soon felt uncomfortable. Perhaps she had the attitude of "I'll try anything once" and then realised she didn't want to, and so that was that. It didn't matter to me now, though. I couldn't have cared less, when all I wanted to do was kiss her, feel her and make love to her, over and over and over again, throughout the night.

Weeks went by and we often found ourselves excited about planning our next weekend together, when we were both child-free. I started to fall in love with her. Not just for the nights we would plan, though the thought of having a line, waiting in bed naked for her, was literal ecstasy, in which I would sigh out for her, "Omg, OMG!" While those instances were breathtaking, so were the moments where we were sober and hung out.

I fell hard and we moved in together.

She was so incredibly beautiful. She wore these glasses and, whenever she took them off, my heart melted like butter. But it was more than that. She was so affectionate. The way she would hold and caress my forearm, she was so gentle, so loving, and so good to me.

There was just one problem; my shallowness! I hated this one little observation of mine.

You see, I enjoyed keeping fit. The one thing I was proud of was that I look good naked. She, on the other hand, had a bit of a belly & didn't really look after herself. For me, it brought back feelings about how insecure my ex was, albeit in a different way.

Now I can admit, I was also modelling my expectations on the women I had seen in porn. My view was, admittedly, biased towards a certain body shape and frame. This filled me with the false sense that I could do better, and it is with deep regret that I felt ashamed of her. The irony of it, for the shame was on me for thinking that all along, never mind the baggage I carried with me!

On top of this, we were both raising our kids. Raising another person's child is never easy. Her son came with his challenges. Looking back now, I wish I had been more compassionate, after understanding my own conditioning, growing up. He unfortunately envied my son, which was difficult to deal with, & brought about arguments between us. I felt like my time with my own son was precious enough, without creating problems for him that felt out of my control. I can imagine he wished it was his own dad, sitting there besides his mum. From my perspective, his dad wasn't a proud father and that might have also made him jealous of the relationship I had with my son.

It caused several confrontations between all of us, as we had different parenting styles and beliefs on how to raise children. I was firm, for example, and said it how it was. She, on the other hand, didn't want a fuss and just let things slide. At times, I had to intervene, and although I had good intentions, I had far from a good attitude. As a result, she would resent the way I handled things.

In time, this led her to believe that I resented her son. The suggestion couldn't have been further from the truth, and the implication hurt like hell. I responded, saying I found her son's behaviour difficult to deal with, that was all, especially when he would kick off and go on for hours and hours, crying for his dad. She knew this; I had held her through many nights, to comfort her anguish and lack of control over how her son felt. But she wasn't buying it. Interestingly, even though I expressed my genuine feelings, and she listened, she still came to believe I resented her son, regardless of how I felt or what I had said. We moved on, but it left a wound that would only come up again in the future.

During this time, my “habit” didn’t help. I would find any excuse for it, especially on my free weekends. Friday night was all I could look forward to, having fantasised about it all week. I now know why. My job, for one, was very physical and I always pushed myself to earn more, so that was my release. Plus, my escape for pleasure remained and, as I had no friends, getting on it was also my way of having fun.

By now, my partner wouldn’t get involved with it. She didn’t like it that I went into the lounge and locked myself away. It became an unhealthy obsession that worried her, until it started to affect our relationship.

Our relationship had started off on good terms. We had a great time in all areas of our lives; we were really happy and never argued. She was my better half, comforting me about my own problems, like not seeing my son as much as I would have liked and arguing with my ex. She understood; she had compassion. Finally, I had someone who could see and understand me. I felt heard.

But she would tell me there was more to life than drugs and sex. How right she was! Although I couldn’t see it, I was conditioned to still use every excuse to escape into my shallowness and indulgence. While she was happy for me to do it – it couldn't have been nice for her to have to support that. And so, those insecurities about not feeling understood started to creep back in, no matter how lovely and supportive she was.

I don't mind admitting that these have so far been my biggest regrets in life. She was so lovely, and I hurt her so much with my habit of wanting to get high. Some nights, when I would leave the house, to avoid bringing attention to myself, I imagine she would cry herself to sleep.

Alongside this habit of mine (and as a consequence), I also had mood swings. At times of confrontation, not only did she feel uncomfortable addressing the problem, but I would have only bitten her head off, even if she raised it kindly. After all, this was all I knew. For me, it was one of my favourite hobbies that masked my worries from work and life in general.

Then, my mood swings started to bleed into our other conversations.

She was having problems at work, being taken for granted and not being offered a pay rise, despite new members of staff getting paid more than she did. Most of the time, she would come home, moaning about it. I would always encourage her that she had an amazing personality, sounded professional on the phone, that she was very smart and could do better, if she looked for another job. But one day, sick of her moaning, I told her that she needed to stick up for herself and have a chat with the boss. That if she wasn't willing to face her boss, ask for a pay rise, or set her boundaries, her lack of courage would lead her nowhere. She burst into tears and took it as though I didn't care about her.

I was devastated that she took it to heart. I was only trying to help, by being honest! I thought of how her projections were hurting me and how, once again, my opinion wasn't valued, when I explained myself and tried to comfort her.

Looking back, I realise how selfish this perspective was. We were both battling insecurities & projecting them onto one another, which made us both uncomfortable.

The arguments began a while later. I'd shout at her at the top of my lungs, which killed me. I'd then compose myself and calm down. I had the ability to observe and know I was in the wrong for yelling, but when she would make excuses for me or sugar-coat things, it led me to raise my voice again, out of frustration. That little voice in my head wanted to be heard, needing her honesty, and so I would go on and on.

All I wanted was for us to openly communicate and listen to one another. Her excuses and silence, however, infuriated me. The irony was, I was full of excuses for my behaviour in the first place and was unaware of the damage I was doing. All she was doing was reflecting it back to me! I couldn't acknowledge that at the time. All I could see was that I wasn't accepted for myself and that our relationship was based on conditions for each other.

I just had no idea the person I was supposed to be yelling at, the person I was desperate to actually hear, was myself.

So why is it that I raised my voice through the roof tops, when it killed me to do so? I've never been one to enjoy confrontation. I mean, I'm all for a healthy debate. But, with my fear of not being seen or heard, raising my voice was a failed attempt at a cry for help. I needed honesty, I needed to feel like I was safe, I needed protection really, and to feel like I mattered.

The truth of it was that I had low self-esteem.

For as long as I can remember, as you have read for yourself, I have been made to feel like I can't trust my thought processes or my emotions. It's no wonder I was somewhat delusional. Worse still, I looked for validation and measured myself, based on how others reflected it back to me. Family members seemed to always be the ones to bear the brunt of it all. After all, we often use those that are closest to us as our punching bags.

If you struggle with anxiety or low self-esteem, as I did, consider taking on activities, such as yoga or boxing. You need a way you can release your frustration now and again. If you don't do any sports, I would highly recommend starting. I took on both yoga & boxing when my life started to take a turn for the worse. It's the best thing I could have ever done, and something I wish I had done much sooner.

Another little exercise I would recommend begins with the saying, "When you start the morning well, you win the day."

Set a routine and, for the next thirty days, do it before you go brush your teeth, for instance. Write out three reasons how having amazing self-esteem would benefit you and improve your life. For each of those three reasons, write out how it would feel to notice that you are getting better and better. When you then go and brush your teeth in the morning, ask yourself, "How can I make today the best day ever?" Smile! Then tell yourself to have a wonderful day!

Whatever challenges arise for you throughout your day, be mindful not to moan to any colleagues or friends, and also be mindful of your thoughts and how you feel. Remember what I said in chapter nine, step two? You are responsible for your life, you are responsible for your thoughts, you are responsible for your own development, and you are responsible for the results you get.

Most of us go to bed and end up going over all our troubles before we go to sleep, unaware that it is at this time that we marinate and prime our subconscious. So, at the end of the evening, go over any challenges you might have and write out the polar opposite of whatever that may be for you. The best outcome is possible in all situations if, at the very least, you consider it. Look into whatever brings you closer to peace and makes you feel happy. Go to sleep with a smile on your face.

For the next thirty days, repeat the exercises. By the end of it, you may need a telescope to look back at how far you have come!

CHAPTER ELEVEN: DAMAGE CONTROL

That lovely woman and I ended up with notice to leave the property we lived in together. It belonged to her son's grandparents (on his dad's side) and I got the impression they, and her parents, didn't like me. One time, she received a text message from the grandmother, with a picture of a devil having its way with a woman, the implication being that I was the devil. The text read that the sex may be great but that was all I was after, that I would ultimately suck out her soul.

I was a shady character in their eyes, & I had inevitably brought attention to our relationship. The nights earlier on, where we were up to all sorts in the night, snorting line after line and having sex, couldn't have helped.

We also didn't get on with the neighbours upstairs, too, so we had to go.

By this time, I had lost a lot of weight. My drug habit meant that I wouldn't eat for all sorts of hours and my self-image reflected how withdrawn I really was. I was ill, from the inside out.

We moved from a maisonette into a bigger property. A whole house to ourselves was an exciting time for us! It's worth noting, when we met, I was only earning £390 a week. I had fuck all to my name and any money I did have, I was putting into my career, van tools, and – of course – drugs. But two years into our relationship, I had started my own business and now made close to a thousand pounds a week or more, with overtime.

All the responsibilities in the new house were mine, as I was the only one able to afford this for us. Of course, in my eyes, this was obviously my responsibility, especially as, by now, we had conceived a beautiful daughter together.

Alongside also having a wonderful son with another woman, this meant that ten percent of my wages were contributed towards child maintenance, & another twenty percent to include towards tax. Regardless, I found the means to pay all the expenses.

I also brought my fiancée a newer car, as a means of better transport for our baby, as the car she initially had was too small and had started to break down. Everything was on my shoulders, to be the provider. I wanted to feel like I could protect my family. But being my own boss, as a plasterer, came with its pros and cons. The cons being that, most of the time, I was owed money, and so the pressure as to how I would pay the bills was always there.

To make matters worse, Mkat had been made illegal in China, where it was produced. Rumour had it that anyone found making it could face grave consequences, and so the market went dead. I could have taken this as my window of opportunity to knock my habit on the head and change my ways. Instead, I ended up substituting Mkat for cocaine. Remember, Mkat was one tenth of the price of cocaine, so by now, I was paying nearly £250 for my drug habit twice, if not more, a month. My financial obligations didn't need that sort of pressure, which meant that whenever I found my feathers ruffled, I would storm off in a huff.

But I had gone from not being able to afford shoes for myself and being the worst version of myself, to turning into the provider. I even started to put on weight at this point and bulk up on steroids, to turn into the protector my fiancée and daughter needed me to be. They helped on the outside, but inside, they didn't. I would struggle so much at the gym, feeling uncomfortable in my own skin, as I went from one machine to another, changing weights. It didn't matter what I did, I hated myself for feeling so withdrawn and insecure. Furthermore, the steroids only made my anxiety worse. This made me more temperamental, which didn't help, given the mood swings I was already having, because of my drug habit. It was unbearable, living with the self-talk & self-esteem issues I had going on, internally.

Money was the only saving grace at the time. But when we would argue, I would throw it in her face. I would use money as an excuse, as if to say...where is your respect? It hurt like hell when she would scream at me that all I cared about was money.

"Come on, give me a break. I pay for everything!"

Besides, I thought, how would we even cope without it? Worse still, I felt taken for granted. My job was very physical, and I went the extra mile if I could, for us. It was exhausting, but I would always ensure she got more than she asked or needed.

Looking back now, how could she have respected me? If I hadn't had the drug habit, things would have most likely been far different. If only I'd had a better attitude!

Before I move on, it's worth noting that, at this time, I still didn't have any friends of my own. All I would do was work and be around my family. We made every effort to see our families and other relatives, but whenever I didn't have my son or when she made plans to stay out with friends...I would indulge myself with drugs, eager to exploit my wild side with sex, and excited to have the house to myself. At the time, my state of mind during this drug addiction was so bad, I was unaware of the danger I was putting my family in. A family I was trying to protect. I didn't even consider the damage it could do, especially concerning the children, if anyone caught on to what I was up to.

One night, while I was indulging, I felt like my home

was being broken into. Then I heard the neighbours mocking me.

"You should be ashamed of yourself; we know what you're up to!" I heard one of them yell.

Paranoid by now, I felt like prying eyes were either watching me or prying ears were always against the wall.

My comedowns were the worst. I would smoke cigarettes like a chimney, in meerkat mode again. By now, I was starting to hallucinate. Tilting my head, my heart would sink and my jaw would drop, trying to figure out if what I was seeing was real or if my mind was making it all up. I would see little aliens hovering around the lounge in their tiny UFOs. Now and again, an entity observing me would move around, so I would follow it with my eyes, and then nod at me, as if to acknowledge its awareness that I could see it. At one point, I also saw a menacing figure from across the hallway, staring at me, smiling.

I'll be honest, sometimes I felt like I had been possessed, to do the things that I did. Some nights, I found it terrifying. Were these entities the ones possessing me to do these things, I would think? I felt ashamed, like I was some sort of laboratory experiment. Especially as, on one occasion, that is exactly how it seemed in my mind. It was as if I was in a holographic room, so to speak, caged up in an imaginary reality, one where I was being watched. This is so strange to wrap my head around now, especially as we go further into my journey and you learn about my experiences with DMT.

Anyhow, this one night in particular, the paranoia of our house being broken into really alarmed me. The lock on the door had fresh scratch marks, as if it had been forced open. Our spare keys had also disappeared. Part of me knew then that we had to go. It turned out our contract for the year was up, anyway. The place had needed a lot of maintenance, after a winter where the boiler broke down on us several times, and it felt like as good an excuse as any to leave.

We moved again to another property and this place was just perfect for us. I made a promise to not indulge at this house. I wanted to show my family how much I cared for them, how much it meant for us to be happy. So, I sorted the deposit, and I furnished the house. Whatever we needed, I worked hard for. I always put everyone else first.

Until the cravings to indulge came back.

At first, I didn't do drugs in the house. Instead, once in a blue moon, we would get a hotel room. This was exciting for us, although that desire I had, on drugs, for that whole-body-multi-orgasm still plagued me. I had been chasing it for close to five years now, and at the height of it all, she would never entertain my desire for the experience.

And so, the nights in the hotel room would turn into discomfort with one another, by the end of the night.

For me, I would do anything for her, in and out of the bedroom. I had shown her that, in how I provided for our family. Why wouldn't she do the same for me? I felt like she never had any intention, if it was "outside of the norm" for her, even at my request, in the privacy of our relationship. She knew what my late-night lounge lock-ins were about. I talked to her about my obsession, hoping she would understand. Instead, she would tell me there was more to life (she was right). And despite my efforts, I still actually wasn't giving her the stability she needed as a mother, due to my love affair with drugs.

I firmly believe, if I had experienced those sensations I was craving, I might have been able to put a lid on it and move forward, leaving the drugs behind. Saying that, mind you, there is a probability to consider...who was I kidding? I was chasing the dragon for that high and euphoria. To this day, nine years later, I have yet to experience that high I chased for so long. I still battle with it, to remain disciplined and have integrity with myself, to not get fucked up. At the time, though, I blamed her lack of understanding. It ultimately led to the destruction of our relationship, only months after moving into our new property.

I went back on my word. She found out I was doing drugs in the house while she was away. It was obvious, because she would call and I would avoid answering the phone. I couldn't speak, with a massive lump in my throat from snorting that stuff. She knew. Why else would I have otherwise ignored her, call after call, text after text? Lost in my own world...

When she arrived home one afternoon, after having gone to the gym, I was snappy and I gave her attitude about the thermostat for a reason I can't recall, other than feeling stressed out and overwhelmed. I'd been on the phone for the past hour to a client who owed me a substantial amount, the bills were due to be paid in the next few days, and I was losing my mind. They had never replied and I was furious at how another man could mess around with a family man with bills to pay.

She was infuriated with me that I lashed out at her, rightly so. I just wished she hadn't taken it so personally, especially as I had expressed the reason for my frustration. I tried to be apologetic, as best as I could, although by now, I was starting to get angry with her lack of understanding at how I had been feeling about the situation before she arrived home.

Were we starting to resent one another? All this time, not having addressed the elephant in the room came at a great cost to our relationship.

During the argument, I approached her to give her a cuddle and calm the situation lovingly. The swift change of attitude must have spooked her. She flinched away from me, as if I was going to hit her. I had never put my hands on her, the whole time we had been together. I felt betrayed and disheartened that she didn't know how much she truly meant to me. I thought she didn't love or trust me, if she didn't know I would never intentionally hurt her, no matter what.

It turned out that another man had previously hit her, and that was where her reaction had stemmed from. But even with compassion for her experience, the fact she thought I would do the same crushed me. I felt angry, anxious, confused, and hopeless. Meanwhile, she felt resentful that I was putting all of this on her.

Raising my voice only made things worse. She threatened to leave me and said that she wasn't putting up with my abuse anymore. However I would express my truth, how I felt didn't matter. She felt like she wasn't being cared for and neither did I, by her. Was this a reflection that neither one of us cared about our own selves, so we couldn't be there for the other?

I could never understand it, in the heat of the argument. I was always made to feel like I was the one with the problem. She also contributed towards the argument, when she would say she didn't want to argue.

"As if I do," I would say. It only made me feel more anxious, patronised, and upset.

All I wanted to do was address our issues. Sometimes, I would bang on about it all night and it would infuriate her. I, too, was infuriated, knowing all too well that it wouldn't get resolved. The truth of it was, I would make it all about me and couldn't see, at the time, how insensitive that was. I should have left it alone.

Actually, I should have addressed my own issues. I had, for example, at one point, gone to a Narcotics Anonymous meeting. I should have gone more than once. If only I had healthy coping mechanisms for how to better understand and express my emotions. Not only was I making it about me for so long, but by now, I had problems. What I really needed was to talk. I grew up always kicking the dirt under the rug, as if the problems didn't exist. So, when they resurfaced over and over again – in my relationship with girlfriends, parents, exes – I wanted to talk it out, as a means to not repeat the mistakes of the past. I just didn't know how to communicate that at the time! Worse still, I didn't know how to end my own recklessness and was in denial.

By the next day, we had both said sorry, but the damage

had already been done.

Which leads me to consider a story about perspectives.

Imagine if I took a group of people to the beach for a road trip and asked each one how they felt about the place. I would get a different response from each person.

One person might respond, "I could cry tears of joy, this is my happy place. The sun kissing my skin, the waves rising up the beach to kiss my toes. I feel refreshed and invigorated; I would love to own a home somewhere near a place like this."

Another would say, "I don't like it here, I would rather be up in the mountains with the snow. I'm starting to feel really anxious with this heat."

My point is that no two responses will be the same. We all have different perspectives, and each perspective is right, if you are standing in the other person's shoes.

Now, put the couple of this chapter in the perspective story together, leave them to argue their differences, and what benefit would be gained, exactly? The road trip would be spoiled for everyone and arguing wouldn't get them anywhere. Arguing never gets anyone anywhere, if you aren't willing to see another person's perspective. It's not about being right, it's about understanding.

We have a habit of reasoning from our own perspective, based on our own experiences, without considering the other. We believe 'this is shit' and 'that is shit' and, before you know it, we are covered in shit, complaining how much it stinks! Well, it's no wonder, wouldn't you agree? And the worst part about it all is that we point the finger at others, but that very finger curls back and ends up pointing right back at our own selves, with issues we haven't dealt with.

In this game of life, you will come across many challenges and learn how to overcome many obstacles. One is how to effectively navigate your terrain and commune with others. So, when an argument or a difference of opinion appears...consider this. What if the other person's response was right...as well as yours? If we are all made of Source or God or the Universe, and everything is perfect in its own divine right, then their perspective is, too. Can you see the God in them and in their actions? What does their perspective offer you that is *for your benefit*? (Because there always is one!)

This is how we begin to get along with one another and live harmoniously. When you live by this way of thinking, the world ceases to be complicated and you will get on with others more. Not only because you are more considerate and compassionate with yourself, but with others also. We then all become free to play our own individual games and, most importantly, rather than dispute our differences, your way of being might just influence another to see things differently, and vice versa. Play your game of life your way, play it well, and if others want to join in – great! Play on. But don't let it affect your game.

CHAPTER TWELVE: MISCOMMUNICATION

Now, you might recall, my fiancée's son and I had had our problems, although I didn't think it was serious. You know, just little things, like I would want to treat everyone to freshly homemade burgers and he would refuse to eat them. His mum would tell me to "just let him be, let him have whatever he wants." We would end up in an argument in front of them. I felt belittled and made to feel as if I was in the wrong, for having a backbone.

I should have left it alone, although I also understand where I was coming from, so far as where creating healthy boundaries are concerned and setting an example. See, perspectives.

One evening, I was left with her son, as she went off to work. She had woken me from a nap after a busy day at work with a "hey" and a kiss to the lips.

"There's pizza and potato wedges to cook the kids for dinner, ok? I'm off to work."

By the time I made dinner, I had completely forgotten what she'd said and called up to her son to come downstairs. As with most young children, he didn't come immediately.

"Dinner is ready!" I yelled for a third time.

When he came downstairs, he looked around the kitchen, in the drawers where the snacks were kept, then went by the oven, stared at the pot, as if there was nothing over there, then looked at me as if to say, "Where is dinner?"

What are you even thinking? Just sit yourself down at the table, I thought.

He just walked back to his room. By now, I was seeing red.

"CAN YOU COME DOWNSTAIRS, FOR FUCK SAKE, AND SIT DOWN AND EAT?!"

I should have been calmer, as I expressed myself. I should have asked him questions, rather than patronise him for his attitude, so he felt better understood. I should have communicated with him in the way I wish my parents had communicated with me as a young boy. But we don't know what we don't know, at the time.

"I've had enough of your attitude. All I'm trying to do is feed you!"

I had completely forgotten that he had been expecting pizza and potato wedges, as his mum had promised and asked me to sort out for the kids, before she went off to work. I'd had a quick nap and forgot and ended up cooking a stew. No wonder he had seemed so confused at first.

Instead, my anger made him try to leave the house. On trying to force his way out and run, I grabbed him, pulled him back into the house and locked the door. The boy threatened to call his dad, the police, and yelled at the top of his lungs. As did I. When he threatened to make his mum leave me, I didn't know how to process it and threw the tea from inside my cup against the wall in frustration.

I called his mother at work, alarmed at how out of control our argument had become, and asked if she was able to return home, as I was very stressed and worried. Her son had already tried to run away before. When she arrived home, I explained the situation and she went to talk to him. The three of us all talked it through, him with his mum, me with her, and then him and me together, to have a heart to heart, as I tucked him into bed. I apologised about the food and reasoned with him that we shouldn't be like this with one another. As for the threats, I had heard it so many times before and was used to it by now. I assumed it was empty talk.

The rest of the week passed by and, at the weekend, he went to his father's. Late on Sunday afternoon, my fiancée received a text from the father to say Social Services had been called and that her son wouldn't be coming back to us, until the allegations had been investigated. Apparently, I had pushed him and hurt his leg, pinned him up against the wall, thrown hot coffee over him, and been abusive. I was shocked. We'd left on good terms when he went to his dad's. I couldn't believe the cheek of his lies or the fact that his dad hadn't asked us what had gone on.

The number of times this boy had come back from his dad's, crying about how bad the relationship was with his dad was, and the lack of attention that he felt, said it all. We always did our best to get his dad to recognise how his son felt and what he needed from him by his cries. Admittedly, he and I had never got on since day one, as he would always give me attitude in his own way. He would make us feel like we were in the wrong and, worse still, that he didn't believe our concerns about his son's behaviour were necessary. But over time, and with effort raising awareness, it had seemed to improve the relationship. This news came as a devastating blow.

Naturally, my fiancée was in tears. Her father was with us at the time, but he didn't say anything. Perhaps he felt it wasn't his place.

"Let's go and get him right now," I said. "How dare they act like they care about his welfare, when he's come back to ours crying, and now has the audacity to say we are the irresponsible ones?!"

Part of me, writing this now, is sad at the above statement. I had no right to talk, I was so irresponsible with myself. How I wish we had all just come together, to work it out for the children. How I wish we had all worked on bettering ourselves, to be better examples for them.

My fiancée didn't feel comfortable taking assertive action, and with no one to back up my plan, days went by. I thought it made us look like we didn't care, that the allegations might as well be true. But we had to wait for Social Services and there was still no sight of her son.

I had just finished work when the Social Service representative arrived. I barely made it to the appointment on time and, I'll be honest, I didn't like the rep, from the moment we met. Here was this stranger, who had no idea of our way of life and the realities we faced every day, who was judging us on what he could observe from the end of his spectacles, making surface level observations.

I found the questions he asked unquestionably undignified, but to my horror, my fiancée was playing right into his hands. I thought, surely the allegation that hot coffee was poured over his head would be enough to prove the information provided was false, given that the boy had no burns or injuries to support the allegations? But no.

When the representative asked if my dad had punched her son on one occasion, mentioning a situation in which he had been given a light smack for being disrespectful (admittedly it was not his place), I left the room. I had no patience for the way the "facts" were being distorted and taken out of context. My parents had always gone out of their way to make us welcome, feed and entertain us as best they could, whenever she and I would visit with the kids.

"Antonio, come here. We need to sign this," she called, to bring me back in.

I huffed under my breath.

Walking into the room, she handed me a piece of paper she had already signed.

Essentially it read: *should we ever feel concerned for your children's safety and well-being, you will be investigated, and we will intervene. Sign to consent.*

I absolutely refused to sign it, on principle. To me, it was basically like saying, "I'm not fit to be a parent and you (Social Services) have the right to make that decision." I was totally shocked that she had signed it, without talking to me in private about it first. If anything, it should have been a mutual decision. If not, we were bound to argue about it later, which would inevitably cause more undesirable problems between us.

The representative left and I couldn't look at my fiancée; I couldn't be near her. At the time, I couldn't understand what was going on or wrap my head around her decision. Even expressing how I felt about it was as good as talking to my own self. Looking back now, I can see that she was fearful of losing her son. At the heart of it, I believe we lost each other that day. Her at the expense of her fear for her son, and me feeling neglected for my own opinions on the matter.

Hours later, I held her, as she lay crying in bed. My mind wandered off, panicking about how we were going to fix this, as I stared into oblivion. What could I do, what would become of us? She must have said something, and I missed it. She lashed out in retaliation, saying I was making out like I wanted to give her support and attention, but that I didn't really care. That broke my heart and really angered me, truth be told. I tried to explain to her where my mind was, but she was in her own world of hurt. Who could blame her?

I hit the bottle that night and smoked like a chimney. She asked me to stop being silly and come to bed. How could she not see that I, too, was suffering? I necked the bottle of wine for comfort. Our life together was falling apart before my eyes.

The following morning, I woke up moody and gave her a half-hearted cuddle, as we were still both raw from the night before.

"I love you," she said. "Have a good day."

I walked away, looking at her with so much sorrow. I

really felt for her. Having kids that weren't both our own together wasn't easy. But I was starting to feel a deep disconnection. We were no longer seeing eye to eye on anything, and I was left wondering if she only loved me only because I offered her financial safety. After all, she never made me feel wanted and never made a move on me in bed. I would rarely hear a compliment

I thought to myself, "I love you so much," as I looked at her, walked out the door, and went to work.

I really struggled throughout the day, with everything playing on my mind. On my way home, I felt nervous, because she was never the type to address anything, unless I bought it up. She would rather act as if nothing had happened. I worried if I said anything at all, that we might argue. Not once throughout our relationship did I feel safe to openly talk. I wound myself up into a proper state.

"How was your day?" she asked when I arrived home.

"How was your day?? How about, how are you?"

That was my unfortunate response in anger. I wish now that I'd told her how I had struggled through the day, rather than retaliating. I was already anxious about arriving home and seeing her, knowing all too well that she wouldn't want to have a heart to heart. I was terrified she would no longer listen to me or hear me out. My worst insecurities reconfirmed. If only she knew.

Before we knew it, we were in a heated debate. I brought up the previous night and Social Services, but there was no real talking. I was made to feel like I was in the wrong for thinking and feeling as I did. The nail in the coffin, however, was when we spoke about the moment I held her in my arms and how it upset me that she would think I didn't care for her.

"Well, those are the facts," she replied. "That's my perception, so that's how it is for me."

I was infuriated. What about my perception? I felt like my account had no credit! Surely, you can see I'm upset? Why does that not mean anything to you, other than for you to take it as an attack on you, as if I hate you? That's what I thought. I became defensive and raised my voice to the top of my lungs, the more she showed no signs of understanding, and made no effort to reason.

She made her decision right then and there, repulsed by me, even as I begged her not to go, walking upstairs to go grab her stuff. I followed her. I found myself feeling helpless and unnoticed, as she walked out the door, with our daughter in her arms. As I saw her leave through the back gate and get into the car, like a sack of potatoes, I dropped to the floor. I remained there for hours, crying my heart out, still shouting my anguish and suffering through the rooftops.

After a while of lying there, I had to pick myself up, as my son was waiting for me at my mum's. I cleaned myself up the best I could and headed over there, not wanting to let my son down, although knowing all too well it would have been better to have remained at home. I arrived and parked up at the front, but couldn't find the will to go inside. The fear of letting my son down, of him seeing his father in pieces, stopped me. I messaged my fiancée non-stop instead, begging her, which didn't do me any favours.

I bombarded her with messages, which was unfair of me. It didn't help either of us; she just read and ignored them. I implored her to talk to me, that I couldn't cope, even while I was with my son, to see that her son had finally managed to drive us apart, like he had threatened to do. Which made me feel like a fool, as if a child could threaten an adult or be manipulative and determined to break us apart.

Three days went by, going through so many emotions and all sorts in my head. The only friend I could rely on to open up with would tell me to leave my fiancée alone, that she obviously wasn't worth my time, that he and his Mrs had been through hell and back, but not once would they dare break each other's hearts.

I saw that she was online and decided to block her from

all my social media, after leaving one last message, with a threat that it was over, right before collapsing to the floor with regret and anguish once again. I couldn't take it anymore. I was torturing myself. She had read the messages, but I hadn't heard any response. I was desperate and, I guess, trying to protect myself.

"You are killing me," I wrote in my final message. "I don't know if someone has stolen your phone and if that is why you are online. The worst thing possible is that both you and our daughter have been in a crash perhaps and are dead. You are with her, so I need a response, please. I'm worried. My heart can't deal with the hurt."

"We are safe and won't be coming back," she replied.

I didn't know how to behave; I didn't know how to function. Was this a mirror of how I actually felt all along? Abandoned? By others? By myself? Was this all resurfacing because I had brushed it under the carpet for so long? Or was my life just unravelling, as it has been for a while, because of everything I had done: the drugs, prison, my addiction to sex, all my insecurities...

To think that only weeks before the whole show unravelled, I had been thinking about telling her that, if she wanted to leave me, that would be ok. I was such a shadow of myself, I lacked so much confidence, that I had been beginning to think that she was too good for me. I loved her so much that I felt so vulnerable, and I was completely reliant on her to love me and make me feel safe and wanted. I had been fragile for so long...

I couldn't call my family; I couldn't call on anyone. Everyone was making out like it was all my fault, that I was the only one with issues. I couldn't talk about myself, and everyone would instead bring up my partner. Everyone was against me. Although they were right about one thing – I was accountable for myself! But what of others, I thought?

I can say that now, as I write this, I clearly had a victim mindset. I had a bad relationship with myself, and a bad habit of retaliating, when others mirrored it back to me or pointed it out. The addictions didn't help. But I knew, even though I wasn't perfect, that I had a good heart and I meant well. I had just never acknowledged, or even known, that everything had to do with attitude and, for what I think and how I act, I am responsible.

And because I didn't give myself the comfort, support and attentiveness I needed – I didn't receive it from others. I knew all along, deep down, what I needed. So much so, that when it was pointed out and made obvious in my life, it was painful. Being told I had no concern for anyone else was only more frustrating, because that's ALL I had concern for. Everyone else, NOT myself. I needed to work on it the other way round.

The ironic thing was that it took me being a provider for my family, while being the worst version of myself, to them all leaving, for me to actually step into my best self, so that I could provide for them in a healthy way. All the while, they kept looking at me through the same lens, because they hadn't changed themselves.

At this point in my story, with no safe space to open up, my anger was a cry for help, as I continued to shout from the rooftops for attention. I went for days, weeks, months, crying at home, crying at work, crying from the moment I woke up from the nightmares I was reliving, to crying myself to sleep at night, every single day, for weeks on end.

As you might imagine, now and again, I turned to the one thing I knew would mask the pain all too well. Getting high and indulging in pleasure was my little treat to myself and a means of escaping the pain. However, the pattern of paranoia repeated. The comedowns at the end had me sitting there, staring at the night out the window, feeling like I wanted to die, at the thought that my now-ex and family would be laughing and shaming me outside with the neighbours, at the noises I was making.

So, let's stop for a minute and explore what it takes to have a strong, healthy relationship. We're led to believe that a "normal" relationship means to always be happy, have zero conflict and be perfectly and evenly matched with each other. This couldn't be further from the truth. Instead, I believe it requires forming healthy boundaries, as well as building compromise. We ought to dedicate ourselves to personal development, have patience, show courtesy and when required to do so, sacrifice our ego, so as to allow for growth. At least, that's what I believe, in my world.

And when it comes to love....what is love, really? Can you define it? Can you solidly spell out things that will 100% answer; yes, this is love? Take a moment to give it a go now. Like the perspective story in the last chapter, what love means to you will be different to what love might mean to another. This will be an insightful exercise, if you've never considered this before.

If you are struggling to answer this for yourself, it's ok. You're not alone. Many of us don't know what love means to us, either. It's why we're often confused and why so many relationships break down, because we're looking for the answers outside of ourselves.

Why else do relationships often go wrong? Would it be fair to reason that, perhaps, it is because we put on a tough exterior, often as a means of protecting ourselves, that we lose the ability to connect with others? We think the tough exterior protects us from getting hurt or feeling vulnerable, but actually it STOPS us from being fragile enough to feel and connect with another. There's a big difference between being tough and being strong, while using discernment.

Love isn't always going to be intense, passionate, or exhilarating. It's also about mutual trust, respect, and partnership. A mature, healthy, relationship requires time to blossom and to grow, but the difficulty is that we live in a world of instant gratification & same-day parcel shipping. We're not used to practising patience. We are often guilty of wanting something, but not prepared to put time into it; i.e having heart-to-hearts and being transparent enough to express what we want and need.

Sometimes, those chats mean patiently waiting for the other person to feel comfortable opening up and coming to an outcome together. Often, if we don't get an immediate response, we rush in and rush out in a tantrum, treating relationships like a toy instead of a treasure, & dismissing all that is good in front of us, in favour of the easy option.

Ever heard about good things coming to those who wait? We usually want things cleaned up right now, resolved, over and done with. How I wish I had known this before; to bide my time and, most importantly, wait for the right time, so as not to add any more tension into the relationship. But I let my head rule my heart and there I was.

Do you let your head rule your heart? Do you let your

fears keep you from being happy? When people build too many walls around them, it can be hard to reach them. Being clinically logical over matters of the heart may result in never fully being able to feel love, because sometimes love is completely unexplainable and illogical. It's why most of us have a hard time describing it, as you might have found from the exercise I asked you to do.

Love means taking a leap of faith. You need to put aspects such as time, rationality, and practicality on the back burner. Allow yourself the freedom to feel, no matter the complications of opening yourself up wholeheartedly, with authenticity and transparency. But in order to do that...you have to make time to be in a loving relationship with yourself.

CHAPTER THIRTEEN: REUNITED

For as long as I can remember, I usually only saw my son every other weekend, and that's if his mother and I weren't ranting at each other. It just so happened that, one week, when the forecast was awesome, I had the opportunity to have both my son and daughter at the same time. I took time off work for this, especially. I was so excited to see them together and hang out as a little family!

As usual, the drop-off was the worst part. I always argued with my son's mother. Now my daughter's mother wanted nothing to do with me, either, and it made it ten times worse. I just wanted to talk. When I saw her, my heart broke all over again. I could have easily fallen to my knees.

She, just as my ex did before her (and anyone else who knew me, come to think of it), knew how I could go on and on about my point. They weren't entertaining it anymore. I would get ignored and, as a consequence, I was left to pick up all the pieces of me that littered the floor, feeling distraught.

When I had both children for the week, I cried in front of her when she dropped off our daughter. I sobbed that I couldn't cope. 'Please' was now my new favourite word around her.

"I will take our daughter back home with me. You are clearly not in a fit state to look after her," she said, after I told her that I was alone most days in the house we used to share, that I missed them all terribly and that I was feeling suicidal.

I was crushed beyond belief, and after a heated exchange, she left, after giving in on leaving our daughter in my care, but yelling that she didn't care about me anymore. Thankfully, my son and daughter were indoors, playing with one another, and didn't hear us. One of the neighbours, having heard our argument, came over and held me as she drove away. I cried my heart out. I did my best to clean myself up after that, for the sake of my kids, and thought I would be better off taking them with me to my mother's. Although, if I'm being entirely truthful, part of me was wanting to give chase to my ex as she sped off. I loaded the kids into the car, hoping to catch up with her on the way to my mum's.

To my surprise, I found her parked up at the local shops. I will always regret what I did next. I pulled up behind her, so she couldn't leave, and I walked up to the car window.

"Look, I know this is not the right thing to do, coming at

you when you just left. Please, please hear me out," I begged. "This is too much to bear; I am suffering. The last thing I want to do is argue, and I know that's all we do, but there is no talking, and I am not alone here, having this argument with myself."

Her response was to say she couldn't care less, and that I was the reason for all the difficulties with her son. I fucked with his head, she told me.

I stumbled back in disbelief. After everything I had witnessed over the years, after all the times she had asked for help, and I'd provided support as best I could, as a father myself. I was to blame? I could not believe how her perception of me had shifted so suddenly. Especially considering the time we had spent together, over the course of five years, who we once were to each other, and who we were now.

Had I been calm and rational, and playing the perception game, I would have been able to see that she was in survival mode. And here I was, blocking her in, quite literally, so who else was she going to get defensive at and blame? Of course, it was going to be me. Her world had also tumbled down, just like mine had.

At this point, the police arrived, pulling up behind my car. My jaw dropped to the floor. How could she? I wondered. But my distress when she dropped off our daughter, having heard I'd been having suicidal thoughts, had alarmed her and triggered the call for the police.

"I love you. Family don't do this to one another," I said.

I talked briefly to the police, my guard up. I told them we had recently broken up and that we were having difficulties. I confirmed that I was alright and that we were off to go see my parents, which seemed to reassure them, so they soon left. I drove off too, feeling like the scum of the earth. I parked up as soon as I had the opportunity and cried my eyes out. My poor children sat in the back of the car, along for the ride.

Arriving at my mother's afterwards, it took a great deal to calm myself down and be present with my family and the children. It didn't help that, every time I looked at my daughter, all I could see was her mother's face. I escaped most of the time, smoking like a chimney outside or upstairs, crying. Most of the time, I was messaging her mother, only to be rejected over and over again, then ignored.

Hours later, we went back to my house. It was soon time for us all to rest and so I bathed the kids, ready for bedtime. It had been one hell of a day, but I finally felt excited for tomorrow. I woke up feeling blessed, with both my kids in bed, still sleeping like angels. I got up, pulled the curtains aside, and saw that the sun was shining. It looked like we were going to have a beautiful day, and we did!

Each day with them was phenomenal, even though most days, I didn't cope well, missing my ex and even her son. Of course, you are always going to miss something that you are so accustomed to. But, I thought with gratitude, at least my kids weren't fighting. My son and hers had never really got on.

During the week, my daughter started developing an inflammation in her intimate parts. I worried that it could be down to poor hygiene or perhaps she was wiping too hard (she was newly potty trained at the time). On one of our days together, we had also gone to the beach, and I wondered if playing out in the sand, under the heat for all sorts of hours, might have contributed towards the irritation. By now, she was crying with discomfort, so I texted her mother and some other women I knew with daughters, for their advice.

"It can happen from time to time," they reassured me. "Go and get some cream from the pharmacy." So, I did.

The end of my week with the kids came and my daughter was still crying that she was in pain, despite my best efforts with the pharmacy cream. I dropped her at her mother's and later heard that she had taken her to the hospital.

A few days later, while at work, I got a call from Social Services. My daughter had been in and out of hospital and was waiting for a couple of other doctors to examine her. That bloody sand, I wondered, under the heat all day long at the beach, couldn't have helped. I also wondered if I should have made sure she wiped with wet wipes instead of regular toilet paper, and that she was wiping the right way. I felt that parental guilt any parent knows, wondering if I could have done a better job.

"Your daughter is under investigation and the police have been involved," the Social Services lady at the end of the phone told me.

I was mortified when she went on to say they suspected that perhaps something had happened under my care.

"Are you happy to talk about it?" the manager asked.

I hung up the phone and cried my heart out, screaming at the top of my lungs, throwing tools all over the place, shouting, "WHAT THE HELL JUST HAPPENED?!"

The lady called back, and I knew better than to hang up again. I had to act responsibly; I knew how Social Services worked now. After all, they were only doing their job. I agreed to talk, though, like any parent, they knew I was upset at the thought I was being accused of being negligent.

The phone call had thrown me, but I was at work and had to act normally, stocking up on material and so on. But on returning to the van, with the material loaded up from the merchant, I turned the key and reversed full throttle into a brick wall. Half of it smashed down. I had lost my mind for a moment, with no idea what had just happened. I alarmed the staff and one of them approached me. I gave them my details and left, in total shock. I went back to work with the materials and then drove straight home.

Later that day, my client called and said the neighbours had complained about my outburst. This was all I needed. Thankfully, the merchants, whose brick wall I'd smashed, never called for compensation.

I was so angry and hurt, at my ex and the system once again. Of course, they were actually offering support and chasing the concerns of the doctor, my daughter's mother, and the other authorities who were getting involved. But past experiences had coloured my judgement and I was scared stiff that they were going to take my daughter away from me.

"The only allegation that has been made is the one coming out of your own mouth," my ex told me.

That was hard to hear. To her, she was only helping her daughter. It was nothing personal and all avenues were being looked at. From my perspective, however, being required to be further investigated was a bitter pill to swallow.

Eventually, when all the facts came to light, the case was dropped, and my daughter received the treatment she needed. It turned out to be nothing more than an inflammation. Relief overwhelmed me. On top of everything I was battling, this was one of the most horrifying experiences to go through. I wouldn't wish it on any parent.

And still, despite the investigation's result, I didn't get to see my daughter after that, for several months. Communication between me and her mother had been poor before, but now it was pretty much non-existent. At one point, she blocked me from all social media. I couldn't text or call. I don't blame her; I was very emotional. My only means of being able to communicate was by email, in which I was too sporadic, impulsive, emotional, depressed, and hopeless. I couldn't communicate effectively and even though I would pour my heart out, the reply was always along the lines of I was better off saying nothing at all! If only I had more respect for myself, but there was no way to dignify this construed mess. I would scream through the rooftops some more. At the sight of all my tears and the snot bleeding out through my nose, I would think, "How is all of this coming out of me?" I never saw puddles like it on the floor.

Despite trying my best, it hurt to realise that the only

thing I could do was give my daughter and her mother the space they needed. It was with the deepest regret that I realised all I was doing was suffocating them.

What it turned out to actually be was the perfect time for me to get to know myself – not least because I had no choice in my life, now independent and on my own. I needed to learn how to communicate effectively. I felt so misunderstood, with no connection to anyone. It was no wonder, of course, because I had no connection with myself. I was discouraged, from my fights with everyone, thinking that I had little support. Despite my efforts, I couldn't see my daughter, her mother didn't believe I cared and had moved on, and I had to grieve my hurt feelings alone. I did not feel safe.

I was being given a really clear sign now. This was my chance to give myself that support & safety I kept begging everyone else for. I embarked with determination on my new mission, in the hopes it would benefit those I loved, & myself.

I started to wonder why the same patterns presented themselves with the two women I had loved. And why did I, too, behave in the way that I did? Why did they both switch off their emotions towards me and behave as if we never had history together, let alone children? What was it I believed had resulted in my children's mothers using the children against me? Was I a bad parent, after all? Did they feel they had to protect my own children from me? Was it because I wasn't protecting myself from my own demons?

Most nights, I dreamt that my ex and I would talk. She would turn her head in disgust and ignore me. The worst dreams were when she was dolled up, with a new man. The attention I needed all this time was now another's and he had more than I could ever dream of, not only spending more time with my daughter, but on the receiving end of everything I needed and deserved for myself. I would let out a loud sigh, waking myself up, talking loudly about what I was going through, then burst into tears.

The days at work were hell. I was fearful of losing all my clients, as I would spend some moments in a corner, crying out loud. Returning home, I would have memories flash before my eyes. Now and again, I'd notice that she had come into the house with the spare key.

Anytime I would go to the kitchen, I would look through the plain glass of the door, into the gap in between the gate at the rear, hopeful that I would see her car where it usually was. As if she was home. It wasn't there. I was alone; I wasn't dreaming. Some of her stuff was still left behind, and for my own peace of mind, I had to hide everything and keep the kids' bedroom doors shut, also.

I had no right to be mad; I had no right to feel upset. I

had no rights at all. The only thing that felt right was ending it all, then and there. Ending my life became my new fantasy. I would toy with the idea of how I would go about doing that to myself. I wondered if a knife to the throat would do it. I imagined it vividly and the idea terrified me.

At the end of each chapter, I've given you many tools that can help you come back to the truth of who you are, and all of these would help in the suicidal situation I found myself in. But when you are in it, really in it, it can be hard to address the fact that you have created your own reality. And that, at any moment, you can change it.

My reality was always to argue between myself and family members, when in times of need and distress, saying that this person isn't listening or that person doesn't care. That this person offers very little support, because that's the habit my neurons would fire and wire along. On top of that, I - like everyone else - was addicted to the emotional response that fire-and-wire reaction gave me. So, I repeated it.

Pretty difficult to wrap your head around, wouldn't you agree? All I ever *wanted* was to be part of a happy family. One where we high-fived and had each other's backs. But that wasn't my reality, so I had to get really honest with myself. I had to put myself under the spotlight. I had to ask myself, am I a victim of my own reality or am I a champion?

The thing about putting yourself under the spotlight is that it comes with pressure.

Like when the full moon is out, the light from the moon actually means that the plants and trees don't sleep. It puts them under a tremendous amount of stress, not giving them that chance to rest. But then — after the pressure of the spotlight, the passing of the full moon, and the chance to rest — they wake up more vibrant than before.

That's what I wanted to do for myself and that's what I want for you, too; to become a more vibrant version of yourself. To reunite with a truer version of you than the one that exists in your current reality. How can you do that? By working on the higher faculties of your mind.

Step 1 - Write out the situation you are having difficulty with. Put the spotlight on it. Get honest about it. Bring it to the light of day. If another person is involved, play the perspective game and journal about what their experience is. What might they have to say? How do they feel?

Step 2 - Acknowledge. Do you get defensive in this situation? Do you retaliate? Do others mirror this back to you? If you were in full control of yourself, no matter what the outcome, and just an observer of your life...how would you be acting?

Step 3 - Rewire those neurons. Use the power of your intention and imagination to meditate on handling that situation differently. Remember, your mind does not know the difference between imagination and reality. Rewiring in a healthier way of being for next time is far better for you than going over a past experience you can't change.

This is a practice and, like a pencil, we need to sharpen these steps, these skills, over time.

It helped me to understand that it first starts in the mind and then imprints to reality, like a new seed being nurtured. Albert Einstein once said that to approach the same situation, expecting different results, is a sign of madness. So, let's change how we approach things we want to change. Use these tools and give it a go; overrun that programme you have going on in your subconscious, and become the champion of your own reality. You and your family owe it to yourself, and one another.

CHAPTER FOURTEEN: THE NIGHT & THE RITE OF PASSAGE

While I was working on myself, my sister moved in with me, which had its ups and downs. She'd also just been through a breakup, and it was neck and neck between us, to see who had it worse. Naturally, I thought I did. She called me out on it.

One day, she handed me her copy of a book by Deepak Chopra. It was the first time I had heard of him. She asked that I read it and so I did, every night before I went to bed. I found myself fascinated with the concepts of spirituality, how by applying spiritual law to life, we gain a better perspective and thus live a more fulfilled life.

This led me to want to explore the subject further. I became obsessed with figuring out my own life. I picked up another book and, this time, another author made me realise I was living with a victim mindset, compromised by circumstances. The book used concepts such as meditation and described the anatomy of our body in a way I hadn't ever known about. It suggested that our heart emits a frequency for up to eight metres, and that is only what the technology we now have is able to pick up and read. It also mentioned energy centres called Chakras. I was blown away by the stories about people's experiences throughout life and how they changed for the better, by working on these energy centres. How they had come to understand how your thoughts were not your own, just static noise that had been picked up over the years. The book also shared how we also have up to seventy thousand thoughts each day and that the majority of them are negative.

The one thing that stuck out for me in the book, however, was the importance of setting good intentions. How we ought to fill our hearts with love, to willingly and fully forgive ourselves and others, and how we ought to count our blessings and be grateful, not the other way around. This was how to stop thinking as a limited body and have an abundant mind instead.

I started to put these teachings into practice, going to sleep, wishing my ex the best. I forgave her, even though I would then cry myself to sleep.

The funny thing was, this wasn't the first time I had come into contact with spiritual concepts. It was just that, most of the time, I was off my face on drugs, in the para-psychological sense.

For example, before my sister moved in, I got a few grams of cocaine to enjoy myself with. Once again, around 10pm, the paranoia set in and I just didn't feel safe at home. I felt like I was bringing attention to myself, off my nut, up to all sorts. I decided to leave the house, but I couldn't drive, so I thought I would go for a walk in the woods. I think I felt safer with that concept, off grid with no one around for a million miles and no worries in the world.

I found myself getting lost. I noticed that I had begun hallucinating and was also hearing things. I felt like I was walking over soldiers in the pitch dark at one point.

"Pew pew," I heard. "I got you."

I scratched my head, walking further into the woods, feeling like some sort of ninja. The sequence of my steps made me feel like I was navigating it perfectly, as if I was missing all the soldiers I was close to stepping a foot on. It felt surreal.

At the bottom of a hill, I found myself drawn to stop. It felt natural to want to sit down, and so I did. Looking into the distance, I saw a ball of energy approach me from afar. The fear resumed and the red energy ball I saw took on the outline of a person. Before it got close to me, it disappeared, as if it had headed off, back in the direction it came from.

I looked around. I felt like I had teleported to another dimension. I wasn't accustomed to the surroundings I was experiencing. It *was* dark, in all fairness. It felt as if what I was witnessing was something very ancient, unfamiliar. I thought I was amongst something you might see in a strategy game. There were axe beings to my right, ninjas behind me. Soldiers strategically placed everywhere. The moon looked as if it was an entity looking down on me, observing me. I was a stranger in someone else's land. It was their home turf, with them all in defence mode.

To my left, inches from me, there were three (what I can only call) Marines. I could feel their presence. I wasn't scared, I was amazed. I could just feel that the Marines were the ones not to be fucked with, if you get what I'm saying.

I humbly got up, feeling like I was trespassing. If I'm honest, I was a little spooked out. I gave my blessings and walked away. I felt as if one of them tried to trip me and I heard a snigger. I walked off, to find myself out on the street and heard what only sounded like monkey noises, as if I was being patronised. Part of me felt like saying, "You what?!" and wanted to go back in and confront whatever was going on. Then fear hit me, and I said to myself, "Don't go there."

I walked off to my left, but I was going the wrong way, so I proceeded to turn around and run. I came across a £5 note on the floor and heard a "Cha-ching!" in my head. By now, it was as if I was playing a game.

I had the instinct to run, and so with that, I ran, and I ran. I started to feel the heebie-jeebies and felt as though I was being followed. When I would stop and turn around, I could see what looked like a transparent body or two, not far off behind me. It was as if nothing was there, but I could see the outline and body of energy it was emitting. I carried on. The moon looked false, synthetic somehow, and around me, there were guardians everywhere. The lights looked like entities of their own and very much alive. I was baffled and couldn't quite believe what I was seeing.

I kept running and thought about putting a hand down my trousers. I thought, by doing that, it would feel like I was fucking, with the motion of me running. I was off my head, I admit, and we know by now that particular wire is fired up for pleasure for me. I heard a voice say, "No, no, no." It felt like the voice guiding me through this moment was asking me to prove myself to the gods.

Running felt like the most natural thing to do, and so I ran my heart out, following all the markings and outlines. To me, it was as if there was something else, other than me, that trained here, and tonight I was following his lead, feeling just as fit, sharp, and agile. To my surprise, I felt as if whatever was observing me felt I was worthy. I ran and ran, and I was unstoppable. I ran like nothing in my life before and got a kick out of it. It was amazing. I felt so much pride, like I was some sort of warrior in training.

I came by a hospital and, again, the lights all felt like

entities of their own. As I looked closer and wandered off, in my mind's eye, I could see that there was a battle going on, light against dark. There weren't many of the light beings left, I noticed. Whatever war was going on was at a great cost to many.

I then proceeded to keep going. I walked further up and found myself at the park, looking at hopscotch markings. I found myself having to choose who I was and from what place I came. I looked at the hopscotch markings on the floor and positioned myself in second place. I would have chosen first, but felt respect for something unknown to me. I honoured that feeling that something was far greater than me. I heard both boos and cheers from out of nowhere. Some as if to say, “Who the fuck do you think you are?” The rest were pleased and welcomed me.

Then, from across the distance, I saw a wolf. I felt drawn to approach it, but felt intimidated by its size. Given the distance, I would have said it was about ten feet tall.

I decided it was best to go back home; I must have run seven miles by now. My legs started to give in to cramping, so when I reached the hospital, I used the bench to stretch out. I had the feeling I wouldn’t make it back home. I was dehydrated!

I ran when I could and did my best to move in a motion that would be most natural for my muscles to engage with my movement. I made it a mile, when I noticed a lady out the front of a house, smoking a cigarette. I approached her with a croaky, hard-to-talk voice.

“Please, may I have some water?”

She flicked her fag and ran back into the house. My hoodie on, white dust under my nose and piercing bloodshot eyes must have scared her off.

I continued walking. As I was looking, to my left was a house with empty milk bottles on the porch. I heard the church bells ring, a couple of houses away. It must have been midnight by now, if not closer to one a.m. A lightbulb flashed in my mind's eye, and I ran for the door, thinking, “Aha, someone is up, someone will surely be able to help me out and offer me a drink of water.”

I banged on the door several times, but nothing. I then proceeded to the back and knocked on the door there also. Again, no response. I recall looking across the grave behind the church, staring into oblivion for a moment. It felt eerie.

As I walked towards the front of the church, I noticed a tap from afar, quite close to the ground, by the flowers. I ran for it, washed my hands, and tried to cup my hands to drink the water, although I wasn’t getting anywhere near enough. Another “aha” moment and the empty milk bottles flashed before my mind's eye, in front of the house I was looking at when the church bells rang.

I ran for a bottle and noticed something odd. A bloke was lurking around, with his hoodie up. He looked shady. I couldn't help but get the impression he was following me. All sorts flashed across my mind...what if he had a knife?

I walked slowly back to the water tap, making out like I wasn't worried about him. I took my drink in gratitude, filled up the bottle again and ran. I was, by now, physically alright and able. Though, the scariest part for me was thinking the man was following me towards the hilltop, with no streetlamps. I ran for my life.

I finally made it home, safe, and thankful to make it to my bed.

They say a man dies twice in his life. One is the death of his ego, the next is the death of his body in this lifetime. That night was the beginning of the death of my ego, as I realised my full potential. That if I put my mind to it, I'd be unstoppable. I ran for all sorts of hours and felt like a warrior. I had already put in the miles and come a long way. And this analogy beautifully ties into my life story so far. The experience that night made me believe I was — and am — so much more than just this body. That there is so much more going on than my mind can perceive.

Spirituality is something we can't fully comprehend. We're accustomed to experiencing our reality with only our five senses, but the perception of spirit doesn't exist in the five senses...and yet, many of us have felt it. It is part of you, as it is of me.

So, the lesson for this chapter is to look back on your life and consider; what was your rite of passage? Where has the unknown indoctrinated you in life? It's time to see yourself as your highest self and expect the good for all. To show courage, show strength, and show conviction. You are capable of so much more than your current reality dictates.

CHAPTER FIFTEEN: THE AWAKENING

Clearly, drugs were a big part of both my trauma and my awakening into a spiritual being. I just couldn't make sense of it at the time. As you've read from previous chapters, I was starting to experience what I can only describe as psychosis and witnessing paranormal activity.

Whether it was seeing short grey aliens with big heads and black eyes, or feeling like I was being watched and running to the kitchen to grab a knife that I took to bed with me, the drugs left me a frightened mess. The visuals I saw were static but clear as day, and would leave my heart racing. Top that off with a comedown when my anxiety was through the roof, it was no wonder I was in a daze, unaware of what to make of each experience.

The day after I went for that run in the night, I went on Facebook and came across a random post about DMT. DMT is otherwise known as Dimethyltryptamine, which is a psychedelic. Now, the difference between this and the stimulants I had been using (cocaine and Mkat) is that stimulants make you feel energetic, euphoric and heighten your senses. A psychedelic, however, makes you feel like your sense of space and time is altered. It gives you feelings of insight with clairvoyance, your sense of reality distorts, and you experience hallucinations. The stimulants had likely been why I had formed a sex addiction in the first place, or had contributed to it, with the sensitivity it enhanced in touch and feeling going through the roof, not to mention the euphoria and release of dopamine.

My experience with DMT would be very different.

This DMT post I found was on a random plasterers' Facebook group that read, "How do you measure success?" I didn't often go through comments, but I found myself drawn to look and noticed a comment that said, "Try DMT and you will soon come to know that success is all but an illusion."

I was curious. I felt like I knew what DMT was. Perhaps I had heard of it from a documentary when I had been fascinated with the unknown, in my early days. Perhaps it was at the back of my mind, hidden away unconsciously, and that's what raised my interest when I read the comment. Perhaps my innate self was screaming out to me. Who knows?

All I know is that I commented to say, "No way, I've always wanted to try that."

I immediately received a notification on Messenger, asking me if I smoked cigarettes, which I thought was odd.

But he was happy with my reply to say I did smoke, as apparently DMT was pretty harsh. He put me in touch with someone he knew who supplied it and, within days, I arrived home from work one afternoon to a package. I proceeded to open it with excitement, before I realised I had nothing to smoke it with. I raced down to the convenience store, which I knew sold pipes and bongs. The minute I arrived home, I sandwiched the powder with tobacco, as suggested by my friend online, and lit it up, smoking the lot.

Within seconds, I heard a sound coming from what I can only describe as an altar. I saw geometric patterns in the most vivid colours appear and explode before my eyes. They looked like Aztec symbols and writing. I didn't close my eyes this time round. I was in awe and couldn't quite believe the experience. Moments later, trying to process everything and make sense of it all, I lit up again. This time, I put a little more of the powder sandwiched with the tobacco into the bong and proceeded to light it up and inhale the smoke. Sure enough, as the bloke suggested, this stuff was harsh. I coughed so hard, I blew everything out of the bong.

According to what I had seen online, you were to inhale it once, then exhale and repeat that three times, before holding it in. I went overboard. I puffed and puffed, and puffed some more, until I lost all sight of reality. I didn't know if the bong was upside down or if the lighter was in my other hand. I couldn't tell up from down, left from right. I had the most unusual feeling, as if whatever was occupying my body - my soul - had gravitated out of my body. I felt drawn to close my eyes. As I did so, I went off into what I can only describe as a tunnel, and I was teleported to another dimension. I experienced what I only now know as an ego death.

In this other dimension, I was met by an entity in her own home world, greeting me. From that day forward, that was who I would see for the majority of the DMT trips I had. I would swear to this day that this entity seemed to want to help me. It was as if I would go through psychological surgery each time. When I was with the entity, I was met with nothing but unconditional love.

I would find myself coming back to my body and then crying my eyes out with gratitude. I looked at my hands, as if I was just noticing for the first time that I was alive. I screamed out again in tears, knowing far too well how much I had taken my life for granted. I felt power beyond what I had ever experienced in my life, as if I was God. I felt capable of anything, as if I was destined for more than I had ever given myself credit for. I felt as if everything up until now was meant to be, that my soul had asked for the experiences I had lived up until now.

This became my new fascination. I wondered if I was just smoking a mind-altering substance that would put me in a hallucinogenic state and was no different than a mere dream. I had experiences after opening my eyes, seeing that my hands were made from plastic, for example, and my material world was nothing but a simulation. I had another experience where it felt like another version of me was checking up on me and directing me to listen to my inner voice. My suspicion, however, was that whatever was going on was far too real. In fact, the experiences felt more real than this reality. Every trip felt like I was coming back home.

On DMT, I opened up my eyes and the air was alive. The minute I noticed it, I got up in shock, observing what was going on. I watched the air move from my left ahead of me to my right, as if to show off and give me confirmation that I wasn't just seeing things. Then the air proceeded towards me, until it passed behind me and touched me on my back. At that moment, I sat down and quivered. I wouldn't say that I felt fear. I was in total shock, as if I had come into contact with a ghost. Again, it was rather eerie. I cried in disbelief, with the feeling that I was not alone and there was so much more to life. I felt cradled and comforted. I felt supported.

Going through these experiences showed me what it means to commune with your higher self or, if you will, commune with your own soul. On one of these trips, the entity suggested I start yoga, and what do you know? Yoga means to commune with your soul. From there, I learnt about meditation and started to meditate religiously, every morning upon waking up, listening to guided meditations. This is where it really all began. The turning point. There was no rewinding the clock.

I began to put my hands together and gave grace, from this day forward. I started to realise how unhappy I had been and how miserable I had been for so long. I was now starting to observe myself. I can only describe it as if I had materialised before my own eyes.

Then I asked myself the questions I asked you in the introduction of this book. How is it that I can love you better? How can I make you feel more supported? How is it that I can be of service to you? What areas in our life would you like to improve on? Is there anything I can do to help?

The answers made me cry, realising how little patience I had, with myself, with my family. Even with my children.

One afternoon, when I was bathing the kids, they were playing and being silly, but making a right old mess and throwing shampoo all over the place. I could have yelled at the top of my lungs, I was so upset. But now, the little things no longer bothered me. And so, I smiled and said, "You messy buggers, looks like you're having so much fun." My awareness that I would have previously gone off on one, outraged, with the mess and 'stupidity' really hit my heart strings. I wanted to cry again. No one deserved to be as high-strung as I was. I must have been so hard on everyone all this time, if I had been this hard on myself the whole time, too.

For the first time, I felt proud of my composure. See, I had been filled up with so much love, compassion, and acceptance during these DMT trips, that I was grateful for the life I had and, for the first time, began to celebrate the accomplishments I had achieved in my life. My past was no longer being dragged behind me; it was all irrelevant. I had little care for the opinions of others and valued what mattered the most; how I felt about myself. The truth is that, once I felt unconditional love, that radical acceptance, everything else just became noise.

The interesting aspect of this is, despite the love from my higher self, I still didn't feel safe, every time I tripped alone. For some reason, I thought, if anyone found out what I was up to, I would be in so much trouble with the law. For one, I discovered DMT is one of the most illegal substances known to man. I wonder why? I say this with sarcasm...I came to realise how different our world would be, if the knowledge I'd accessed on DMT was accessible to everyone. I now knew what we were all suppressed from, what had been denied to many of us, all our lives. War on drugs? Try war on consciousness! This is why I didn't feel safe; I felt like I was now a threat to our modern-day society. I became angry with the fact that none of us would suffer remotely as much as we do today in our world, if we only knew the truth and the meaning of life. That we are not lineal beings, but in fact spiritual beings, having a human experience.

The descriptions about good intentions I read before, in books like the one my sister had given me, started to make sense now. To come from a good place was all that mattered; the rest was irrelevant. It was as if I had finally woken up from a dream and broken the spell of smoke and mirrors.

Despite the lack of safety, for the first time in my life, it felt great to be me. I recognised the importance of being present and taking life moment by moment. Not in the past, reliving the experiences and emotions from before. And nowhere near the future, anticipating and imagining what was out of my control. I wouldn't say I was starting to let go and be at peace, because I still wanted to fight for what I believed in. I still wanted to be a loving father to my children and offer them the stability and security to make them feel safe in this world. I was, however, starting to understand and face up to the music. After all, I had done what I had done and there was no turning back the clock. My attitude started to improve, allowing the expression of others to make their own choices, too.

We humans have this terrible habit of predicting future circumstances as being no different to the experiences we have already had before. And we usually make no effort to change them, either, especially if we are forced towards a situation we would altogether prefer to avoid or only get on with it if we have to.

In my case, my ex wanted nothing to do with me and I found myself stuck in a behaviour loop, every time I saw her, when I went to pick up my child. I couldn't help myself, desperately wanting to talk, although she had nothing to say. I would just humiliate myself in public, crying my eyes out. With my new spiritual practice, I came to realise I needed to compose myself, learn breathing techniques, and deal with my anxiety in those moments. Most importantly, I needed to build a picture in my mind's eye of how to conduct myself. (Admittedly, I learnt this through trial and error, so far as managing all the above. It didn't just happen overnight!)

My life began to take steps in the right direction, and I soon followed, by getting familiar with my self-talk. I took up drawing again and dared to pursue a better life. I never knew about self-love. It was something I only later came to discover. The more I got accustomed to different ways of going about things – having a good frame of mind and view of life in general – the more practical my self-love became.

I decided it was time to start enjoying life more, by going on holiday retreats and taking up education. I chose to leave the home I lived in behind me and downgrade into a house-share, to save money. This was a hard decision for me, as I was living by myself and owned everything you needed in a home. I had everything society said I should have, at my age. I was, however, prepared to live in a house-share, as a means to start saving.

Before I knew it, just as I had sold everything, hired a skip, and bought myself a ticket to Portugal, for a surfing and yoga retreat I was excited about, and handed in a deposit to move into an awesome en-suite I had found...The Lockdown happened.

It was all over the news. Spain was in a full-on lockdown, and people in Italy were out on their balconies, singing to each other. By this point, I was starting to worry. Everything I had worked so hard for, my business, what was going on in the supermarkets with toilet paper...all of it.

My parents and I got talking and we decided it would be safer if we all lived together. Seeing as I was going to a house-share either way, I thought this would be a smart move. My sister and my brother also lived there, meaning all the rooms were occupied, so I lived in the lounge, on the sofa bed. It felt wonderful to be with my family, especially with everything going on in the world.

Apart from sleeping on the sofa bed, however. After being accustomed to my own luxury mattress, that was an awful experience. The sofa bed had a thin mattress, and I could feel the metal bars beneath me. Most nights, I was so uncomfortable, I couldn't sleep.

With all the stress about the state of things mounting, and still working on my personal problems, I soon found myself having further problems with my family. They were unable to understand what I was going through spiritually and unable to support me the way I needed, because I still didn't know how to communicate my needs to them. I felt like an outsider, every time I tried to talk to them about my problems; the breakup, for example, and not being able to see my daughter for several months by now. I was really heartbroken.

One late morning, I ate three grams of mushrooms I got through a mate of mine and went out to enjoy a hike. I had taken a small enough dose of the mushrooms that I would ween out before heading home. I was gone for the next several hours, in Mother Nature, before coming back home for a BBQ my mum had arranged for us, later that day. But I'd had such a wonderful time on my own, and felt so enlightened, that I wanted to share it with my mum and dad. I wanted them to experience this, too.

So, at the BBQ, I slowly brought up the subject of spirituality and my fascination that there was more to life than we might otherwise perceive. My dad didn't want to know. We all started arguing and I, once again, felt like I had to be quiet and muzzle down my thoughts and interests. I took it to heart. I tried to reason with them.

"Little do you know how lucky it is that I'm sitting here. Little do you know that I have been contemplating taking my own life, and this is what I have to show for it."

My dad showed no interest; we hardly spoke, as it was.

The argument continued and I was made to feel like I was the problem, once again. Sure, I might have been speaking out of "the norm" and being controversial, but my intentions had been good. I was hoping to inspire and encourage the conversation, with something meaningful. For the first time, I felt like my life had purpose. For once in my life, I was fascinated by what it meant to be alive. I was only trying to open up. Admittedly, I felt frustrated, getting shut down. Everyone else also felt frustrated and, it's fair to say, we all managed it badly. It was a hot summer's day and alcohol was involved.

My dad got up from the table, midway through eating. I decided to go and talk to him.

"Look, I was only trying to talk about some interests of mine."

"No," he replied. "You were trying to impose yourself on us and take over."

I saw red, discouraged and torn, from the inside out. It felt like this man before me was a stranger.

'I don't know you,' I thought. 'My whole family is against me; I'm a troublemaker and they all tell me all I care about is myself, but all they care about is their own selves.'

We were projecting onto one another, but at the time, I might as well have been the enemy.

We began arguing again; I was literally pinned against the wall, and everyone was outraged by my behaviour, making out like I was responsible for their own. As usual, expressing that I was the problem. With that, I had an outburst and called them out on their bullshit.

They told me to leave, told me I wasn't welcome anymore. I was so angry, I felt humiliated. In all honesty, I felt really confused by the whole situation. I couldn't understand how we had all started to argue over me just wanting to share a beautiful moment over lunch, which I had experienced that day. I felt like no one in my family had any time or care in the world for me. Any challenges we faced as family were quickly to be passed over and blamed on me.

I saw my life flash before my eyes, all the recent years, as if I never once mattered. With that, I punched a hole in the wall, grabbed my car keys, and left. I went off to my old property, with nothing other than a blanket and a pillow, smoking one cigarette after another.

I contemplated getting a few grams of cocaine, although I knew it was a bad idea. I knew all too well what I would get up to, making a whole lot of noise and bringing attention to myself. And I knew that, when the comedown hit, I would feel so much worse than I already did. The last thing I needed was to be catapulted deep into depression and driven into shame, most likely suicidal once more.

A few days later, I spoke to my mother and realised my own attitude stunk. Truth was, I was still reacting, rather than engaging.

It's something I'm very willing to admit I still struggle with, now and again. Being conscious takes effort. Being aware of your own triggers and understanding them takes effort. It's an ongoing process.

To be honest, we could always empathise & rationalise

afterwards. But I needed to learn how to do that when it mattered most, in the heat of the moment, or at least at some point during the conflict. Not after the damage had already been done.

By now, I had begun to have more understanding for others and not be so quick to judge or make false predispositions, but everyone was so used to who I had been, compared to who I was now, they were pre-empting my responses. The frustration was real! Especially because they were still the same themselves.

I was genuinely sorry for taking things to heart, though, and I most certainly could have handled things differently. We all could have! I told my mum I was going through a lot, emotionally. She agreed that the current circumstances were not ideal & that what I was going through personally, certainly didn't help, either.

So, I returned to the family home and slept on the sofa bed once more. It was nothing short of bliss. Prior to the argument, I was going through hell on that bed. I was so uncomfortable and could barely sleep, twisting and turning for the sweet spot I couldn't find. But after two nights on a cold floor in my old place, rigid as a rock and waking up in the morning with sore bones...I had never been so grateful. My perception shifted, as I looked around my living space in the lounge and I gained perspective: to be thankful for what I had right now. If not for that, I may have fallen back on my victim mindset, a victim to my circumstances, and made the situation worse. This time round, however, I was a champion!

Have you ever wondered to yourself why we're all so different? Why we have different cultures, different sets of beliefs, and ways of living our lives? Using me as an example; having been rigid in my thinking, only to become more open minded, unlike others in my family. Why was that?

I believe it's because we spend a long time, living in the past. Holding on to dear memories of, 'This is why I am the way I am, deal with it.' Holding on to that story for dear life, until it defines you. Until you can say to others, "You don't know what I've been through!" It's a way to justify our behaviour, ourselves, and the way life has played out for us. To think of all the brutality, wars, and human disasters, just think of the stories we hold on to collectively, to justify our actions to one another!

So, now I want to share something with you that could quite drastically change your life.

It's called Spiral Dynamics, it's a model that was created after research into human beliefs, values, ideals, and overall thought structures. What they found is that human development has this arc to it, like a spiral, thus why it's called Spiral Dynamics. As we evolve, individually and collectively, we go up this spiral. And as we go up, we gradually take on a position of higher perspective.

In some cases, we don't move up the spiral at all. Most of us find comfort, don't challenge ourselves or look into personal development, due to limiting beliefs that tell us not to expect anything different from what we are used to. But the sole reason for existing in the first place is to live, and with that. comes the natural order for us to grow. Think about it; we're babies that grow into adults. Change is our only constant. It's what we learn in that process of change that we can either take and apply to our lives, or we stay stuck at one level.

We can either create or disintegrate, and with that, what I mean to say is: evolution is growth and we should stretch ourselves into new experiences and knowledge. Only then can we evolve and come up with new ideas. Otherwise, we become fixed & stagnated. We often feel "stuck" and miserable...this is the difference between a victim and a champion. Those who choose to change and those who refuse.

Claire W. Graves, who was the originator of the theory that was later popularised as Spiral Dyanmics, said it best, "What I am proposing is that the psychology of the mature human being is an unfolding, oscillating, spiralling process, marked by progressive subordination of older, lower-order behaviour systems to newer, higher-order systems as man's existential problems stage."

In Spiral Dynamics, there are eight primary stages that I want to introduce you to, which will help you understand what level you are at, how you can dive in deeper when obstacles or challenges of your own come up, and how you can syphon out the lessons, move on & grow, and become a more mature human being.

These eight stages are named in this order.

1 - Beige
2 - Purple
3 - Red
4 – Blue
5 – Orange
6 – Green
7 – Yellow
8 – Turquoise

Each stage on the spiral represents a worldview structure, an assumption of how everything works, and the overall rational thinking for decisions being made. Each stage has a preference of dress styles, language trends, popular cultural norms, architectural designs, art forms, religious and spiritual expressions, social movements, economic models, philosophies, and an overall statement about how our lives should be lived.

Now, I could go through all the distinctions in detail, but I thought it best to simplify and stick to the basics. That way, you can use the basic principles to broaden your own understanding and see how it might be applied within your own life.

1: BEIGE

This stage is the most basic, with the fundamental thinking of, "Just do what you must, no more, no less, to survive." At this stage, the individual wakes up every day, concerned with nothing other than how to get by in their day. This would consist of having food, water, warmth and sex. Nothing else would even come remotely to a priority. This individual would barely have a distinct sense of self, only the immediate satisfaction of survival needs and "what is in it for me." Primitive hunters and gatherers, for example, would be at this stage. And you would think that rarely anyone in modern times would be at this stage. And yet, with poverty levels and people constantly worried about money...many stay in this survival mode only. I was shocked to realise that I had lived most of my life at this stage.

2: PURPLE

This stage is where society realised, in order to thrive rather than just survive, they were better off working together...and so a sense of belonging to a community emerged. And since the basic needs for survival were met, there was more time to think about the distinction between cause and effect and understanding why things happened. You can think of this model being formed in older tribes, where there was a social hierarchy. You would have had someone you respected, the chief, who was responsible for the decisions. But everyone else had their own role to fulfil within their community, adding to everyone's survival, as a whole.

For me, this is interesting to acknowledge, as I see it as the collective as a whole; our government, for example, our own family as well, and our own group of friends. What is it that each of us individually have to contribute to one another? How do you see this level through your own eyes? What is your leading role and how does society see you?

3: RED

This stage is otherwise known as the egocentric model. Once the purple stage evolved and the community started to hunt, gather, and explore together, they looked to dominate and cultivate other areas. However, encountering other tribes, you can see the clear sense of distinction between 'us and them.'

This is where the purple and red break away, for red focuses on the individual's needs. In the tribe situation, the individual would be the leader, who would do anything and everything possible to defend his reputation and the reputation of his tribe, at all costs, with very little sense of remorse, paying very little attention to the implications of his actions. Whatever the impulse of his actions, an individual in red will not have a sense of responsibility and always blames others. Red was the dominant force when empires ruled the world and why we have seen so much bloodshed throughout history, when rulers have led from this paradigm. To this day, you can see this egocentric model still governs most countries; the separation of them and us. You can use gangs in this example, as well. They might have remorse for their own kind, but see anyone else as their enemy.

Blimey, you could describe this stage in my life with my own family members, at the worst of times! How about yourself; can you see this in any situation, collectively? And finally, can you relate with red in any aspects within your own life, as well?

4: BLUE

This is known as the purposeful, yet authoritarian, stage. The adoption of religion is a good example of blue thinking. Religion was introduced to unify the regions, but it forced a fixed view on people, creating a very absolute authoritarian society that imposed the code of God onto people. The order enforced a code of conduct that believed what God said is right and wrong, there is only one right way, and any deviations from the path are punished, resulting in you going to hell. In a strong blue society, you had to abide by authority, do right by the code of God, and follow the rules or suffer the consequences. Dogma characterises this stage.

And yet, can you see red bleeding through dogma? Interesting, when you look back through history. Some of the world's most violent atrocities came from blue thinking; The Spanish Inquisition, The Salem Witch Trials, and a lot of the holocaust movement happened because of blue thinking. We can still see that, to this day.

It's interesting to look at, really, because the blue stage is all about morality, to preserve good at all costs, but lacks the perspective of outside thinking, leading to stage red bleeding through. A shame, wouldn't you agree? Can you see the relation to my own life story, where I questioned authority? Can you see it in your own? Where are the patterns of dogma that you are following, or breaking? What are you struggling with, when it comes to rules put upon you?

5: ORANGE

Stage orange is what is known as the prosperity stage, which governs most of the world today.

Individualism takes centre stage, having broken away from the blue herd mentality, and it is all about being free and living the good life. So naturally, democracy, having rights and freedom of expression, came about through orange thinking, as morals were based more on ethics, rather than religion.

Orange places strong emphasis on capitalism and free markets, and views the world with the assumption that there are haves and have-nots. It encourages us to act in the majority interest, in order to have. The pursuit of material pleasures is very strong here. The point of an orange life is to pursue personal success, usually meaning making a lot of money. You might even think that an orange life's report card is based on how much they have got. A person at the orange stage of their life loves to show off all their nice things. The nice house, for example, and nice car, the hot wife, and all the latest technology, etcetera, in order to display this success to others.

Science and rationality also take a strong hold here, and this is very important, because it leads to ground-breaking new discoveries and technologies that have the potential to greatly increase the quality of life and progress humanity in general. This way of thinking also gives birth to a lot of atheists, though religion can certainly still be a factor in stage orange. But it is much less fundamentalist and does not rule one's life, as it once did with stage blue.

The trouble with stage orange is that it causes competitiveness with one another and, although that's not a bad thing, so far as growth is concerned, it depends on how you approach it. You can either come at it as, "Who has the most, who can do the most, look at me, what I have and what I can do" with stage red bleeding through, or you can instead ask, "What can I do to contribute towards society and make us all better as a whole?"

Those who choose the former, and rake in the most money, through the selfishness of wanting to maximise profit, unfortunately create inequality and destroy our planet, using up all of its resources, never mind all the pollution we're creating.

So, I would like to ask you here, what can you do to feel like you have a sense of purpose, to no longer be adding to the suffering of others? What is it that you can do to make the world a better place?

6: GREEN

In stage green, we are much more aware of the suffering of others and the world at large. Feelings, rather than achievements, are what matter, at this stage. Togetherness, harmony, and acceptance drive all decisions. Lots of social justice movements happen here. This is the new age movement, where we see spirituality emerge within socialism and liberalism. The awareness is raised for equal rights and evenly distributed resources, across everyone in all nations. We begin to see the demand for change and that it is about time we start looking out for one another and our planet.

The trouble, however, is that stage green is heavily receptive to group thinking. The pressure is very high, as are the beliefs towards collective decisions, thus breeding dogma. Stage green still demonises lower stages and thinks their way is the absolute right way to go about things. Green thinking, however, is creating a collective victim mindset and causing widespread censorship, if something is not politically correct, in the eyes of whoever is pulling the strings.

Although the actions of stage green are amicable, stage green lacks the understanding of the system of the world, in order to bring about genuine change. This stage is transcended when doubts about the collective mind arise, such as, "What the hell is going on here, why are we all thinking so differently?" Instead of finding separation in your answers, you begin to realise the interconnectedness of everything. How each system balances out the others, and how they all integrate to create the perfect functioning society...much like in nature, when the bugs all have different purposes and yet they all contribute to Mother Nature working in harmony.

How do you see sense in stage green and what does it all mean to you? Can you begin to see how everything ties in together, to form one huge playground for us all, with different elements to suit the needs of the individual? What is your role in this?

7: YELLOW

At this stage, things get really interesting. Stages 1 to 6 are described as a Tier One civilisation. Each stage believes their way is the absolute correct way of thinking. From the yellow stage onwards, it is Tier Two, where we now begin to start embarking on a more level playing field, evolving the collective consciousness.

Stage yellow realises that everything ain't so black and white, where previous stages thought themselves correct and others wrong.

For example, a stage blue fundamentalist Christian would project their beliefs on to red, orange and green and would consider them deluded for not following the way of God. A stage orange, rational-minded fellow, who loves capitalism, will demonise blue, because of fundamentalist dogma, and think their beliefs are stupid and irrational, with nothing to back up the speculation of God, as it is not supported by science. Then, orange would call green socialism stupid, because it threatens their prosperity, individuality, and freedom.

Yellow thinking, rather than demonising, examines why blue fundamentalists are the way they are, why the orange capitalists are the way they are, and why the green socialists are the way they are. Stage yellow looks at the greater system at play. So, when someone at stage yellow looks at problems, they look to find out what is the reason for it, in the first place. When stage yellow looks at racism, for example, instead of cancelling them out, with stage green's cancel culture, they examine why that person is even racist in the first place and they seek to change that system, so no more racism is born from it. Stage yellow consists of looking for solutions, rather than criticising and demolishing, in order to make a greater impact overall. It seeks to look at the bigger picture in life and recognises that society is just a build-up of different systems. It sees that the clashing of the lower stages puts everything in jeopardy. Yellow sees all of society from above and sees that the only way we can all get together is through understanding of it all.

One begins to leave stage yellow, as they develop a greater appreciation of the sheer intelligence that the Universe has and recognises that, to make global change, will require a global effort, collectively.

What are your biggest takes from this, and can you apply it in your own life? How can you individually make an impact at this stage, by realising that we all need to work together?

8: TURQUOISE

Stage turquoise is described as experiencing the wholeness of existence, through mind, body, and soul. You might describe this way of thinking as used by mystics, gurus, and sages. At this stage, deeper levels of spirituality emerge. This includes oneness, whereby we are all one another, perceiving a different reality and non-duality. We are all the Universe, perceiving itself through our own eyes, or there would be nothing altogether, without anything to perceive it in the first place!

The ego here is no longer prevalent and the turquoise way of thinking is concerned with all forms of life. Every single thought and action is oriented towards the wellbeing of all life and not just humanity, in the long run. They realise the intelligence of the Universe will carry everything in the direction that it needs to go; therefore turquoise thinking will only intervene when necessary.

Someone at the stage of turquoise does not learn through observation or study, but by actually becoming and experiencing the very thing they seek to understand. That's how deep their empathy goes. You would think of someone in turquoise as someone such as Jesus or Buddha. They see no boundaries; all is one and they care for and are concerned with everything in existence. They are more or less a pure vehicle of this force, this intelligence that flows through humanity, bringing us all towards unconditional love and higher consciousness.

A lot of stage green or stage yellow people will talk turquoise, but will not embody it, which is what stage turquoise is really all about. The embodiment. Can you imagine what a stage turquoise might look like? How might that feel for humanity? Turquoise's way of thinking would mean no differentiation throughout the planet and equal measure for all. There would be no separation anymore. How do you perceive turquoise? What might heaven on earth look like for you and what can you do to be a part of that yourself?

This is Spiral Dynamics, and this is how we can all individually and collectively grow. Make note of which stage you identify with most. You might find you identify with different stages for different areas of your life, such as; career, family, relationships, education...etc. That's ok. What's important is that we are always reaching for the next level of growth.

Use these stages as a stepping stone to understand yourself and others. Remember, no one individual is ever just one colour. We all have so much depth to ourselves. Remember to understand that we all have a reason for what and why we do things. In some areas, there is a little turquoise in all of us, perhaps there is also a little bit of beige. How can we help one another and how can you also help yourself? That is what we are all here for, to enhance our way of life for the good of all. To all get along, to be compassionate, to show care, even if we don't understand the "whys" of others. To at least try to understand that this, too, is their own life, their birthright to experience.

CHAPTER SIXTEEN: BECOMING ONE WITH SELF

I had a lot of time on my hands throughout the lockdown, and my main thoughts were the realisations I was having about life and myself. It kind of felt as if I was losing the plot, with all the internal conflict I was experiencing, and that with others. From the breakup with my child's mother and not having access to my daughter, I was also battling cognitive dissonance, trying to make sense of all the trips I'd been having on DMT.

On these DMT trips, I was experiencing what felt like communication with entities and angels. I was teleporting into the unknown. On one trip, I had been shown how the Universe was created and that our probability for being alive was close to non-existent. That it all started with chaos, the big bang, one massive orgasm, if you will, that gave birth to all that there is. It was as if I was shown the maths equation of life. One less of a fraction and we wouldn't even be alive.

One day during the lockdown, I received a phone call.

"Hi there, Antonio, do you remember Chris, the chimney guy from that job you did recently?"

"Not really," I replied.

"He asked if he could have your phone number. He'd like to chat, but I thought it best to get your consent first."

"Sure," I replied and thought nothing more of it, for a few days.

Then I got a call from Chris, which I will never forget. I was almost in tears by the end of it. He stated that, if it hadn't been for me, he would have taken his life. He had been planning to for ages, had obsessed over it for some time now, just that he didn't have the guts. He said that, when he met me, he learned two things. One, don't judge a book by its cover. And two, always expect the best out of every situation. He said that my openness was a breath of fresh air. When he met me, he was wary of me, but after getting to know me, he recognised that I was a really nice guy. (I guess I look a bit intimidating. I'm covered in tattoos, for one, and have a 'Jack the lad' kind of vibe.)

To be honest, at that point in my life, I was talking to anyone who would listen to me about my breakup, and all the hallucinations and experiences I was having, whilst on DMT. Speaking out loud was also my way of making sense of it all. I was fascinated to share! I mean, I was teleporting into other dimensions and communicating with majestical beings out of this world, in my head, and so I would tell anyone who would listen. Everyone must have thought I was mad! I sure as hell thought I was losing the plot.

But I was just thankful for the love I would receive on these DMT trips. The experiences were enlightening, and it was all I had, at this point.

I had very little idea how my words had impacted on Chris, until we spoke. He mentioned over the phone that the feelings I described to him, whilst taking psychedelics, encouraged him to take it upon himself and go down the holistic route. He said that one thing led to another and he came across a shaman, who held Ayahuasca ceremonies.

"I am reborn," he said. "If it wasn't for you, I might have been dead by now. I have been closed and had my guard up for so long, feeling like all I am familiar with is pain and loneliness. I didn't think I would ever be capable of getting involved in a relationship again. I didn't want to get hurt again. If not for you, I wouldn't have been able to let go and open up. I have a new flair for life and feel grateful. Thank you so much."

When the conversation ended, I sat there for a few minutes, trying to process his words. I was warmed and touched, blessed and even more grateful, to think that, through all my pain and discovery, I had managed to inspire someone else, or at the very least, influence them down a better path.

It's why I'm now writing this book. I wouldn't have in a million years thought this would've ever been possible for me, especially considering my dyslexic failure in school. It just goes to show that the systems we have in society and the report cards aren't always right about you. Think about what spiral dynamic level our schooling system is built on; that should give you a clue!

The only thing you can guarantee in this lifetime is change.

As Chris and I exchanged words, he recommended that I get in touch with the shaman who held the Ayahuasca ceremonies and, without hesitating, I did. When the first lockdown was lifted and there were fewer restrictions, I found myself journeying up north, four hours away, listening to Wayne Dyer the whole way. Time flew, as if I was only on the road for an hour.

When I arrived, it was such a beautiful home, with a big open-plan kitchen, a big dining table, and a bookcase, filled with lots of books about philosophy. There was a big geometric tapestry that filled the whole back wall, with an altar in the middle, filled with crystals and sage.

I was welcomed with open arms; they all seemed so lovely! We all sat down round the dining table; the shaman, his wife, and a few others. We got to know one another, before the shaman then gave us the lowdown on what to expect. Within an hour, we all gathered around in a circle by the altar, as I had expected, and it was requested that we meditate and set our own intention for this experience, that we open our hearts, open our minds, & embrace whatever unfolded. Mine was to find my own self and heal; I so desperately wanted to heal. We all then proceeded, one by one, to sit in front of the shaman and drink from a wooden cup, filled up with Ayahuasca.

Ayahuasca is a tea, otherwise known as an endo medicine that is widely used by the indigenous Amazonian tribes. It produces vivid hallucinations and profound personal visions. It has been used since the dawn of man, to access altered states of mind for spiritual exploration, allowing one to enter the supernatural world to heal, get in contact with the divine, and gain insight and knowledge. This tea is also used to purge the body, while purifying the mind.

DMT is the freebase that is extracted from the plants they use. But the difference between DMT and Ayahuasca is the duration of the trip. Where DMT lasts for around fifteen minutes, Ayahuasca is for a duration of five to six hours.

After taking the Ayahuasca, we all then sat back on our mats, closed our eyes as requested, and remained in our own space. Before long, we all heard chanting and singing from the shaman, and I couldn't believe my ears.

For most of the experience with Ayahuasca, I wore a

blindfold I had intentionally brought along with me. My intention was to go deep within and gain clarity into my own life. I desperately wanted to awaken as the best version of me. The blindfold was my way of saying, without a doubt, that I meant business. Up until now, the whole experience felt romantic, it felt sacred, and if I'm honest, it was one of the best times of my life to date. I recall pulling back my blindfold at one point and opening my eyes, looking around, smiling. Everyone smiled back at me.

The minute I proceeded to put my blindfold back on and close my eyes, in my mind's eye, all I could see was a white background. Then, it began raining the colour pink. Dancing before me was the most majestic angel I had ever seen, looking at me with a big smile, proud of me, welcoming me in the safety of her space, showing me the kind of love I had been accustomed to whilst on DMT.

How can I even describe unconditional love? It feels like safety, it feels like acceptance, it feels as though you are held in high admiration. I haven't, to date, felt as safe as I did that night; it was profound.

As the night went on, the drums came out and started to play, and all I could hear were cries of joy from the people around me, and the cries of joy from myself, as I joined them. We poured out our hearts, each of us realising that it was ok; this material life we were living right now was all but a dream, an experience within infinite experiences, if you will. And that the pain we endured in our lives was for a reason - so that we might feel and grow our awareness and compassion for the contrasts in the multiverse. We were cradled. We all felt as if we had just been birthed out from the agony that our own mother suffered, with the labour she endured.

Call it what you like; for me, that night, I found God.

There was a lot to process and the experience was emotional and intense. Most of us either purged by vomiting throughout the night or crying. By the end of the night, I didn't sleep too well, as we slept on the floor with thin little mattresses and blankets. I didn't mind, although I was in for a surprise.

The ceremony I went to came in two parts. Day one was with Ayahuasca and day two was with Huachuma. I stayed the following day again, to experience the grandfather spirit, Huachuma. I had thought that the following day would be the same kind of experience, going within myself. Boy, was I wrong. Out of six people, only three remained for Huachuma.

When I woke up in the morning, I sat at the dining table with the others, as we reflected on the night before, over breakfast. Once I came back from my morning run, new people walked in. One of the facilitators excitedly told me that I was about to have the time of my life and that us men, in particular, were going to bond over a magical time of laughter and joy. This did sound exciting, but I was a little confused. After all, I had my blindfold with me. I hadn't come here to socialise; I had come to go within and heal, to find myself. My state of mind was still a mess and my emotions were all over the place. A sense I had felt for so long that was amplified more than ever after day one. It was as if I was in static mode and broken, not yet quite myself.

The shaman expressed the intentions of the grandfather spirit, the masculine. Huachuma had been used since the dawn of man, he told us, especially within tribes that exchanged goods with one another. Huachuma was used to bond; it showed the intentions of a man's heart and that was how trust was built, through the ceremonial act.

We meditated for a bit and offered our blessings for one another, taking turns to approach the altar and drink from the cup. We then went outside to the garden. One of the guests looked after the hot tub, and filled the furnace lit up full of wood. One by one, we went about getting to know one another.

I was really socially insecure. It was a familiar feeling I had dealt with my whole life, feeling like a shadow of myself, with little self-esteem and no confidence. The duration of this whole experience, right out in the open, I felt trapped and vulnerable. It made my insecurities so much more apparent. I hated that about myself. I felt as if I was having a meltdown; there was nowhere to escape, and I was malfunctioning. My mind was going into overdrive over the thoughts of others, as if I could see myself through their eyes. I couldn't even walk; I felt like I was carrying so much on my shoulders, it was like dragging sacks behind me. I walked with shame about how I was conducting myself, I was so insecure.

I felt so uncomfortable with my own self.

Others lay on the floor, laughing and having so much fun, crying tears of joy now and again, in hysterics. I envied everyone so much; I could have burst out crying at wanting what they had. At one point, I did my best to comfort myself by saying to myself, "Have some fun, they are lovely people, stop being so negative." I did my best to try and break out of my shell, but it always amounted to the same hyper-insecurity.

Why was I like this? Why did I feel the way I did? Why was it that I suffered like this for so long? The more I thought about it, the more it seemed like I had been going through life ambivalent, withdrawn from my genuine self, imprisoned in my own nightmare.

"Would you like a piece of chocolate?" one of the ladies

asked me, as she was going through a bar. I mumbled, embarrassingly, asking what kind of chocolate it was. The words coming out of my mouth felt so awkward, I could barely talk, let alone express myself. Then two of the girls called me to lie with them. They cuddled me and I could clearly see they felt sorry for me. Even in their arms, I couldn't relax. I was so tense, I felt as if they could feel me intensively vibrating, as if I was shaking.

At one point, the lads got into the hot tub and requested I get in, too. I didn't want to, at all; I couldn't face taking my top off and getting into my shorts, to jump in with them so closely. I was worried that I might be viewed as gay around the men.

What might they think of me? I was worried they would weigh me up and judge me, based on what I said and thought, how I presented and carried myself - especially amongst the men.

I wondered, once or twice, if perhaps I was bisexual. Was this why I was funny around blokes? Going into my thoughts, feeling into it, the idea certainly didn't arouse me. I might have, on the odd occasion (whenever I was so intoxicated with drugs that I had little to no inhibitions), considered it, but in those times, all I cared about was the pleasure.

I realised I've always been this way around blokes. The

childhood trauma I experienced in this area certainly did not help. I wouldn't have said that I was confused. But it *was* starting to become apparent that I did not know who I was.

I had no education, no self-power and no self-esteem. I didn't know my own worth. I had been carrying around the mess of my life, from my earliest memories up until the present day. This all weighed heavily on me and distorted my view of my own self. That view was toxic, never mind what anyone else thought of me. After all, everyone else's thoughts I was imagining were only my own that I plucked out of thin air and believed to be real.

Having recently started delving down the spiritual path, I found thoughts being manifested as a peculiar concept to grasp. Were my thoughts true? If they manifested and mirrored themselves right back to reality, didn't that make them real? By that logic, these people WERE thinking those thoughts about me, even though I was imagining them.

That's what you call projecting your internal dialogue.

At one point, too uncomfortable to be around others, I took myself up the hill behind the house at the retreat. I wanted to meditate, but felt so confused that I just ended up staring into oblivion, unwilling to escape the madness I was experiencing inside and how little control I had of my own self. Not long after, the shaman followed me up.

"What is troubling you?" he asked.

"I feel guilty for giving everyone such a hard time; I feel unbearable to be around. I'm fully aware of how awkward I am," I mumbled, desperately wanting to open up and get to the core. "When I was young, I had gay experiences."

As much as I wanted to, I didn't have the courage to tell him about the drug problems and the habits that I formed from that, as well. I felt ashamed. Looking back now, it is clear to see I was blaming my inner child for my problems in adolescence.

This was why I was in so much inner turmoil. I had never paid it any mind; I didn't know I had the control and power to forgive myself. I was not kind to myself; I had no love for myself, and thus I continuously insisted that I hated myself. How awful that I thought the relationship I had with my own self was so broken that I didn't care if I didn't wake up from my sleep the following day, and never even knew it.

"What you experienced, as a young man, is normal. You are giving yourself a hard time over something that is natural to all of us, in one form or another. As you have expressed, you were a kid; you both knew no better and it is just a part of life," the shaman told me. "Everyone here has expressed how much of a beautiful human being you are, my friend; you must know this of yourself."

With the shaman's words in my ear, the day after the event, I packed up my stuff and said my uncomfortable farewells, feeling like I had made a fool out of myself and left a bad impression. On the way home, I stopped at a nature resort that was surrounded by a lake, which had been recommended to me, and went for a walk. Boy, was it beautiful. I sat by the edge of the lake, overlooking the water, as I listened to the playlist from the ceremonies of the last couple of days, which the shaman was kind enough to share with me. Listening to lyrics from the song *The Power Is Here Now* by Alexia Chellu, I let out the loudest sigh and cried as I sang along. I thought of all the things I had done; I thought about my family, I thought about my recent breakup, I thought about all the pain I was carrying around, dragging me down. I felt so fragile. It was heartbreaking, but as the song ended, I was thankful for the 'aha' moments life had brought me, especially since the start of my awakening. From that day on, I felt like, even if I could turn back the hands of time, I wouldn't change a thing.

At that retreat, I learned that there is a difference between compassion and empathy. Empathy is the capacity to understand or feel what another person is experiencing, from within their frame of reference. That is, the capacity to place oneself in another's position. Whereas compassion motivates us to go out of our way to help the physical, mental, or emotional pains of another and ourselves. Compassion is often regarded as having sensitivity, which is an emotional aspect to suffering.

Now, if you have two people standing in front of you, one you love and one you dislike, your immediate reactions to both will be different. It will be instinctive. But, can you have the same reaction to both of them? Of course, and the answer lies with compassion.

I'm curious; what if we were to combine compassion with empathy? Now we would have a different kind of compassion. There is a hidden grandness within us, but you have to be prepared to look within yourself, at the soul level, to find it. That love, the unconditional aspect of the mightiest aspect of ourselves, is within reach for all of us. I'll ask you, what would the world be like, if you could look at another human being and see that within them, too?

Have you ever looked at a baby? Have you noticed the way that you look at an animal? You don't judge them, so why, when you turn around and look at others, or yourself in the mirror, is your first reaction one of judgement? When you meet a human or look at yourself, you throw up your guard, don't you? Of course you do; it's that first level of spiral dynamics, that lizard brain part of us, that survival instinct to judge friend or foe. But your brain has evolved beyond that capability now, and you can choose how far up the spiral you wish to go. That is what makes all the difference; that is what I'm talking about.

Do you recall Chris? He said he learned two things from me; not to judge a book by its cover and to always expect the best out of every situation. Wouldn't you agree that it helps to be more open-minded and look outside the box? Chris found empathy in the words I was saying and chose to treat himself with compassion, because of it. Can you begin to see what he saw?

CHAPTER SEVENTEEN: THE MAGIC MUSHROOM CEREMONY

When I arrived home, I felt drawn to look for a spiritual mentor. I now wanted to explore the holistic approach further, implement all my discoveries and embark further on my healing journey. I came across a lady online who I felt drawn to; there was something about her that magnetised me towards her. When we spoke, I found out she, too, worked with plant medicines. One thing led to another and we got speaking about energy centres, our chakras.

For those wondering what chakras are, let me elaborate. And let me start by saying there are more energy centres than just those I am about to describe. But the basic chakra points are as follows.

The root chakra, located around your pelvic floor, is related to our basic survival needs and contributes towards our feelings of stability, safety, support, and grounding. Its colour is red and it is called the MULADHARA.

The sacral chakra, located around your belly button, is related to passion, and contributes towards our creativity, sexual urges, playfulness, joy and desire. Its colour is orange and it is called the SVADHISTHANA.

The solar plexus, located at the bottom of your rib cage, relates to our personal power, motivation and will. It also contributes towards managing the digestive system, which in turn, transmutes nourishment into valuable energy for the body, and thus holds our ability to manifest, too. Its colour is yellow and it is called the MANIPURA.

The heart chakra relates to feelings of love, compassion, forgiveness, connection and understanding. This is the primary chakra - the bridge between the higher three chakras and the lower three chakras - Its colour is green and it is called the ANAHATA.

The throat chakra naturally relates to communication. It's also a place of purification, as it is home to the thyroid gland, which balances the hormones and keeps your immune system healthy. For me, this personally expresses how the importance of speaking your truth, being authentic, and contributing to open communication makes for healthier living. Its colour is blue and it is called the VISHUDDHA.

The pineal gland, otherwise known as your third eye (in the centre of the forehead), is related to trust, belief and awareness in oneself, and that which you perceive in your mind's eye. It contributes towards intuition, wisdom, intellect, knowledge, understanding and your imagination. Its colour is indigo and it is called the AJNA.

Finally, the crown chakra, located at the top of your head, is related to universal consciousness, and contributes towards enlightenment. It is the chakra responsible for a healthy spiritual life. Its colour is represented either as pure white or violet and it is called the SAHASRARA.

I could go on and on about this. There are so many fascinating facts and facets to uncover in the spiritual world, to uncover within our metaphysical body.

For example, we have more than just one brain; we also have an earth star, and so on and so forth. What blew me away most was discovering the Merkabah, which is your spiritual vehicle in this 3D plane, your metaphysical vehicle, your infinite being. That is a subject best explored over a glass of wine and researched to find your own favourite teachers and teachings on what you feel called to learn.

For me, I like to think of myself as a battery. If all my energy centres aren't switched on, I am not working at full capacity or living my life as fully as I could be.

Interestingly, each of the chakras has a colour, and having spent time studying spiral dynamics, I found it ever so interesting how the two seemed to connect. Having studied other information and practises...I wanted to know more.

My spiritual mentor and I went further and spoke about

meditation, connecting with your inner child & connecting with your higher self, as well as all the lessons I have shared with you throughout this book. But the best thing we talked about was when I shared my life story with her. I left no stone unturned, for the first time in my life, with a stranger. Not once did I feel any inclination of judgement. She held space for me and fully allowed me to express myself, as she supported me. I knew I wanted to work with her.

There is so much power in being able to share your story and not be judged for it.

She helped me delve deeper into my spiritual practises and taught me how I could ground myself and connect with myself more deeply. These practises would help me gain much more clarity and insight about my body, who I was and what I was capable of doing. Things I had previously never thought possible.

I knew I still had a problem, though. I told her that one of the biggest challenges I faced was my desire to get off my face, and how I loved to use drugs, with the intention of watching porn, that I loved the pleasure of both combined. I told her how, only days before, I had found myself parked up somewhere in the middle of nowhere, with a few bags of drugs. I felt ashamed that someone might have seen me, that I might have drawn attention to myself.

"Kindness," she kept telling me.

"Offer yourself forgiveness gracefully," she implored. "Do not feel ashamed about sex; it is natural. Did you enjoy yourself? It's ok, what is done is now done, it's time to move on."

She then proceeded to have me close my eyes and go within, to feel my own heart space. She asked me, "How does it feel? Breath into it and fill yourself with love." For the first time, I started to notice how heavy it felt. It took some going to lighten up and, the whole time, she would direct me to speak to my inner child and say the following, "I love you, I'm sorry, please forgive me, thank you."

Having been so supported by my mentor, I started to take an interest in reaching out to more people in the spiritual community. One day, I noticed one of the lads who ran a Facebook group within the psychedelic community was arranging a magic mushroom ceremony. I had been following the group for a little while by now and felt comfortable with him. He was a family man, for one, and had a lot of experience, camping away with others. He said he was going along with his brother and a woman this time. I felt drawn to go, too. I decided I had nothing to lose and nothing better to do for the evening. I felt drawn to go within that night; it was a good excuse to meditate for several hours. I also loved the idea of gaining further insight and perspective into the spiritual world and strengthening my belief in it. (Because, I'll admit, my ego was still fighting to make out like it was all "woo woo" and that perhaps I was just losing the plot, hallucinating. After all, my whole belief system, up until now, was coming under attack and being contradicted.)

It wasn't the first magic mushroom experience I'd had, though. Only months before the shaman trip, I had gone camping with another lad I had met online. I had decided I wanted to experience plant medicine with magic mushrooms for the first time. That night, my heart raced with social anxiety. And I recall the lad asking me, with a frown on his face, "Do you love yourself, mate?"

I felt patronised by him at the time, but I was grateful for the insight, as he led me to start questioning my relationship with myself, in the first place. Wow, I realised, how sad that I didn't love myself, shocked to find out the bitter truth, once I stripped it all back and was transparent and honest with myself. Not long after that, I did magic mushrooms by myself. I put the candles on in the lounge, then turned off all the lights. For the first time in my life, I felt like I could weigh in both my hands how much I loved myself. I felt like I was having a romantic time, enjoying my presence; it was beautiful!

So, I thought I knew what I was in for. On my way to

meet this Facebook lad and his female friend, I called my mentor, to brag about my decision, that I was off camping and having a magic mushroom ceremony.

"How many grams are you taking?" she asked.

"Seven," I replied. "I have all my camping gear, my hammock, the lot. I'm only about an hour and a half away from the campsite now."

She expressed her concern that the night didn't sit well with her.

"Who are you going with? Why seven grams? That is way too much and is well over an initiation dose. I wouldn't even do that much myself and I have worked with them for a while now."

I was already halfway to the destination, by this point.

"Well, you've already decided to go, so you may as well see it through," she told me. "But only take half of that, as that will give you the experience you are after and is more than enough."

After debating over it, I agreed to follow her intuition. After all, that was what I was paying her for, to guide me and use her experience to consider what I should follow through on safely.

I would like to take the opportunity to recommend to anyone considering going down this route, to seek a professional community to take you through the plant medicine process.

I found out the hard way that, for some, this is just a recreational experience. They are experimenting & looking for an excuse to camp out and hallucinate. I would advise, when doing anything like this, to look for a facilitator with experience, someone who has respect for the medicine, who understands shadow work, and is able to hold space for you, because you experience some crazy things on plant medicine!

"Best of luck and namaste," my mentor said. "Please call me tomorrow, to let me know you're safe and how the journey went for you."

I arrived at the location first and didn't have to wait long before the others arrived. By now, it was getting dark. We quickly greeted one another in excitement, took our camping gear out of the car, then navigated around in the dark with our flashlights, as the lady in our group directed us to the location. She had been here before and couldn't wait to show it to us; the spot was supposedly sacred and a lot of others before us had used the area for the same intentions.

We arrived and, sure enough, there was a fire bowl in place and a little table made from a tree trunk, with a watertight container sitting on top of it. Inside the container was a book and pen, where others before us had shared their stories. I looked through it and one story read, "Sorry for taking the book with me. I have been haunted ever since, please forgive me."

"Check this out," I said to everyone.

"Yeah," the lady replied, "this place has history. Apparently, witches live in this forest."

The Blair Witch Project came to mind and I gulped, but I was comforted to read other stories in the book, sharing their memories of enlightenment, farewells, and wishing anyone embarking on the journey safe travels.

We set about camp, then the lady who had shown us there said she wouldn't be staying with us. She felt as though it wasn't her night for it; it no longer felt aligned. Before she left, she made a joke about me getting sacrificed in the fire, but I thought nothing of it and paid it no mind. Instead, the others and I talked about the witches who lived in the area and laughed it off. We gathered up wood, made the fire, and sat around with music.

One of the guys gave me the seven grams of magic mushrooms I had bought from him. I told them I wouldn't be doing it all.

"Why not? We're all doing the same amount."

I should have seen this as a red flag. Even in spiritual communities, peer pressure exists. A lesson I wish I'd known sooner. If your boundaries aren't being respected, you aren’t in a safe space.

I told them I had recently signed up with a spiritual mentor and, after discussing it with her, we agreed it would be best that I only do half. I guess they either couldn’t see my perspective or didn’t support it. They encouraged me to do what I had originally intended and planned with them - the full seven grams.

“We’re all in the same boat anyway; let's not waste it,” they said.

I caved into peer pressure after only eating half of them, looking at the rest, thinking, “That’s not a lot more, fuck it.” My old neurological pattern was projecting through once again, having few boundaries with drugs.

Now, you might wonder why I didn’t listen to my intuition and, instead, conformed. Regrettably, at the time, I still hadn’t formed my own boundaries. I was early in the stages of establishing and developing the fragile relationship with myself and healing. This is why I cannot emphasise enough the importance of building self-love, self-trust and self-care, so you always do right by yourself and not give in to peer pressure. Because, when you attach to the motives of others, you lose yourself and thus you also lose connection to your gut feelings.

We moved on to celebrating together, after that. One of the lads got out his mouth harp and laid another on the table, which I picked up and joined him for several minutes, playing away. Not long after, I started to feel the effects of the mushrooms kick in. My head felt light and spacy, and this out of body experience came over me. I decided to lie in my hammock and, soon, the other two did the same and lay on their own, too. I closed my eyes, excited to commune with the spirit world and get to know myself more deeply, ready for the shadow work and healing.

In my mind's eye, I started to see, from afar, a huge being that resembled an ogre crossed with Godzilla. I said hello and immediately regretted it, as I seemed to have caught his attention. He looked my way and began walking towards me. I was convinced he was well over forty feet tall. I was trying not to be terrified, but my heart started racing and I panicked. I then opened my eyes and had a horrible realisation.

"Fuck, this will go on for a few hours and it's out my control."

I sat up in my hammock, then swung back. I ended up malfunctioning, that's the best way I can put it. I no longer knew how to behave. It was as if I had lost all mobility over myself and felt off-key. I fell off the hammock backwards & heard one of the lads say, "He's on some madness."

I got up and as I looked over to the fire, I realised that a king wouldn't behave this way. I sat, observing the flames, & went deep within my thoughts, composing myself. I felt a power surge through me, as if I was observing through the eyes of a king.

An hour must have passed in the whole experience and then the strangest thing happened. The tree behind me felt as if it were alive. The minute I paid attention to it, I could feel it, as if it was saying, "Hey, just chilling out with you."

My whole view of everything around me came alive, as if everything was an entity in itself. By feeling, I could see the lifeforce of everything around me. It was no different than me, just another layer I could see, aside from my own perspective of reality.

The mushrooms came on stronger, as I looked at the fire some more and began to feel as though I was God. I felt comfortable stepping into the fire; I wanted to. I felt called to be one with the fire and merge, although I instinctively knew better. Even though I felt like that was possible for me, it was as if I wholeheartedly had to believe with distinction that I could do it. However, I knew all too well that my human form would only burn myself. If not for that, I might have jumped in. I started to sense that the soles of my shoes would melt, my trousers would go up in flames and there was no going back from that. The urge was strong to do so, yet I fought it.

I went back into my hammock and closed my eyes. BAM. In my mind's eye, I could see the tree of life. Wrapped around it was some sort of dragon or serpent. The entity started to question me, through my feelings. I was questioned as to why I went back on the agreement I had with my spiritual coach. I had no answer and, instead, panicked. It turned into a battle of there being no alternative, other than to explain myself promptly. I muttered that I had no valid reason, other than not having the will to stick to what I had agreed on. In which case, the feelings replied, how do you expect your spiritual coach to help you in your journey, if you have already broken your word? I felt alarmed and agreed that I should have kept my word, that this wasn't a good place to start, and that, with no trust for one another, there was no honour. How could I expect spirit to work through me, so that I would get the guidance I needed?

I was being confronted and, by now, I was alarmed, muttering under my breath out loud, "We're all born out of our mother and it's showtime." I knew the other two heard me, as they started to laugh.

An hour or two later, I got up out of the hammock again and sat down by the fire, which was starting to lose its flames. None of us had topped it up. I felt called to pick whatever flames were available and cup them in my hands.

I sat down and observed it, flickering in my hands.

A minute must have gone by, and although I could feel my hands were starting to burn, it was as if I was being given insight and revelations about our material world. That we came here to experience the density of love from a higher place of consciousness, with the freedom to choose. Murder, rape, all the extremes in life, were all part of this polarity and contrast with the free will to choose our own experiences. That judgement was nothing but a scenario and a figment of our imagination that we collectively agreed to label, conceptualise as good or bad, and that one would not exist without the other. That it was about consent, through our soul contracts. What we agreed to, before we came into human form. That, at its core, all there is, is love, the freedom to do as you will, that was - and is - our god given right. As this realisation dawned, I threw the fire from my blistered hands in a daze, with what I was processing. I looked down at my hands, trying to work out the problems we face in this world and how we can end suffering.

I then walked onto the fire bowl, as a sacramental offering. Thank goodness no one had replenished the fire. The bowl collapsed and I fell to the floor. The music that had been playing from one of the lad's speakers got intense and there was some sort of countdown, as if a rocket was about to launch. In my case, I was in a panic; the fire was dying and there was little burning wood left. I looked up at the sky and the moon looked as if it was an alien race, observing humanity once again. The fire burning out started to resemble our life force, diminishing along with the flames, in my mind. The countdown of the song, going from ten to one, made me feel with clear certainty that I was being called to save humanity.

I rushed to pick up whatever fire from the floor I could, to keep us alive, but it wasn't enough. As I looked at the lads across from me, with their lights on, the only logical option I could see was to pick up the bowl of fire and bring it over to the light, before the countdown came to zero. I could refill the fire with the light, I thought. I was relieved, but I terrified the lads; they had no idea what was going on.

"All we do is complain, all we do is moan. We're so ungrateful with life and we take it for granted. Let's have a cuddle, come on lads, all there is, is love," I said out loud. I spoke to them with a sense of pride about my realisations of what it meant to be alive, to become one with the essence of life and become one with God, for we are all the living God ourselves.

They hesitated and wondered what the fuck I was going on about. I pulled on one of them to come close to me, but he withdrew.

Before long, my consciousness started to experience the feeling of oneness, I felt as though I was *them.*

Simultaneously, I also felt like I was my children. If I could feel and think as they did, I could communicate with them. I manifested them before me, in my mind's eye, and even called out to my exes with forgiveness and love. "It's all alright," I told them. I felt like I was with my family, friends, and everyone, for *I* was *us all* and *us all* were *all one.*

I was God and I could see the multiverse. Time was an illusion; simultaneously, everything that is, everything that ever was and will be, was happening right now. But the most fascinating aspect was to experience nonduality. I was God, playing all the roles you could possibly think of. As if he were engaging with his own self, with the expression of individual identities, as a means for a dialogue and the free will to think. A simulation with itself.

I have always found myself fascinated by science.

There is a company in Switzerland, for example, called CERN. At their facility, they have a large hadron collider, capable of spewing out incredible amounts of energy. They investigate particles, working out the makeup of all that is life is. Combining this with the realms of quantum physics, the countless studies hypothesising infinite realities that simultaneously co-exist within our own 3D realm, I felt like

I was Neo observing the Matrix in code.

Earlier on in the evening, all of us had been talking about the possibility of the big bang being one massive orgasm of creation. We had laughed that all of us came from an orgasm. Was that the route of all creation, we wondered? After all, the true source of love can only be found within intimacy. From love comes passion, from passion the desire, will and determination to make it so.

All the times I had been to the woods, off my nut on drugs, trying to pleasure myself, crossed my mind. I had so desperately been seeking freedom, to let go without judgement and just enjoy myself. This was the only reason I took myself off in the middle of nowhere, in the first place. I was hoping to find a place off-grid, with no one close by at night to hear or notice me, so I could just be free to BE. Instead, I would always make out like a Meerkat, checking to see who was watching me. How I would have liked to just let go...but I still hadn't experienced a prostate orgasm.

The human in me realised I was endangering myself. I remembered the time I had almost been caught on one of these drug trips and had to hide, before running off to my car, as I was being followed. I started to understand the predicament then, that all it would take was for a group to find me off my head and vulnerable, for me to have been humiliated, beaten, or worse still, raped. How could I live with myself then? It would have been much safer in the confines of my own home, without a doubt! It was only the shame I felt, thinking that my neighbours could hear me and not mind their own business, which made the paranoia kick in, and so I never felt safe in my own home at these times.

The shame that had stemmed from being locked away as a little boy, the shame of being told I was wrong for thinking and feeling as I did, for acting as I did. The shame of all of it, repeating itself over and over.

Anyway, back at this magic mushroom ceremony, suddenly, the music slowed down and it kind of felt romantic. That was the vibe going on. What came next only God himself knows, but I was still under the mushroom's influence, thinking that the alien race was judging us all, ready to extinguish us all, based on my next move. It was as if the scenario I was in right now was meant to be; it was destined. God (if you will) or my soul allowed for this opportunity, before I took on my human form.

All sorts of thoughts started to go through my head, as I battled with them. On one hand, I wanted to make a sexual move on the lads and let go. On the other hand, I thought, “What the fuck? Hell no, what are you even thinking?!” Then the creation of all existence vanished before my eyes, and it felt like a sign from what the God in me wanted to do. I just wanted to orgasm over and over again, into a multi-faceted creation, simultaneously and timelessly, on a loop.

With that, I could see in my mind's eye that I was creating universes. The vision was one that words fail to express, except to say, I was in awe.

"Fuck it, boys!" I yelled. "I'm ready to explode into everything here, now and everywhere into infinity."

The lads looked at me, wondering what the fuck I was on about again. The God in me had very little patience for stupidity, and with that, I took my trousers off and threw myself over the bowl, with my legs up in the air shouting, "Go on, fuck me!"

The lads, stunned, took a step back and laughed. I grabbed the burning wood that was left over and shoved it in my ass, as if to initiate. Luckily, none of the charcoal burnt me. At this point, the lads became aggressive.

As I watched them kick off at me, I stared at them with compassion and understanding. I was them and they were me. The behaviour going on was as laughable as it was predictable. As I was experiencing nonduality, all I saw before me was ego. Their behaviour was childish and expected. I had empathy for them both, as they yelled for me to put my trousers on, but I was frozen and timeless.

Part of me felt as if this whole time was only happening with my own self.

"Do you care about your family?" I asked. "Do you love your loved ones? If it wasn't for me and my inner knowing, I would have vanished you all off the face of the planet and this is the gratitude I get. If only you knew who I was. If only you knew that I've only kept this whole show going, because I love you unconditionally." The God in me spoke freely.

I started to feel the cold & woke up, as if from a dream. I heard them making fun of me, as I put my trousers and trainers back on. I wrapped myself up in a blanket and sat by a tree in front of them, simply observing, as they made threats to tarnish me.

"We're exposing you," they laughed at one another.

I witnessed it, as if it were all a show. It was as if I was watching an animation before me, some sort of holographic play. At one point, they seemed to calm down, but then started to question if I had murdered anyone.

"What an idiotic question," I replied. "Many have lost their lives and there has been more bloodshed than I care to count."

Over and over again, they asked if I had killed someone, they told me that I was dangerous, they called me a public liability. I sat there and asked if they would rather I killed myself, for I wouldn't care at all, if only it meant peace filled their hearts, to find comfort that I would be one less problem they would have to deal with. I was genuinely, in my heart, prepared to sacrifice my own self, out of love for the wellbeing of humanity. I fear if I had a knife at that moment, that I might have openly slit my own throat; that's how much I believed in what was going on.

At that point, I seemed to have snapped out of my trance, thankfully with acceptance in my heart. I neither judged myself nor them. I was at peace and content, and I asked them a simple question.

"Do you believe in God and, if so, do you consider all the visions in your trips to be real or does part of you question it at all?"

"Of course we believe it's all real," they replied.

But when I asked, "Do you really?" and apologised about the night and what was going on, they just laughed.

I stared at them. I wanted to exclaim, "Let's pack up our stuff and go on an adventure." I could see that we all waste our lives, trapped in our environment, imprisoned in our own minds, living mundane lives with repetition, living under the illusion of obligation to the responsibility of having a job or what have you. I really wanted to, for a moment, get up and go, walk to the end of the earth, and experience the full contrast of life. I thought about my children. If not for them, I might have picked up and left. At least, that's how it felt at the time.

Instead, I walked off to my hammock and struggled to sleep, all night in the freezing cold. The next day, I explained myself, shared my story and offered my perspective.

An hour or so later, the lady who had left us originally came to get us, with tea, and I openly told her what had happened on our trip. It wasn't half as uncomfortable as I had expected. The lads laughed that I got up into the fire and she laughed with amazement that I had done what she had joked about - that I would end up sacrificing myself. She said she had felt worried that I was out of control and that is why she had left the previous night, as there was too much masculine energy built up within us all, and that perhaps I was unstable.

Now, a conscious, healthy, masculine, spiritual man - in my opinion - conducts himself with purpose. He is centred. He is certain in himself and his actions, and can provide a gentle, sensitive, open, warm heart space, when required. He is not only here to protect, but also to provide space for the divine feminine to unleash wild creativity. It is safe to say, that night I unleashed a lot of the divine feminine, creative orgasmic energies, rather than the strong centredness of the masculine. This is ok, for all humans are both. Nonduality. And having denied my feelings, and that softer side of myself for so long, of course, it was due to be unlocked.

But take it from the lady - a divine feminine woman always knows when a man is in his centred purpose, for she feels safe and stable in his presence. If she does not, then you are about to tap into the wild energy that she deals with every day! Hold on for the ride!

I walked off into a corner by a tree, feeling like I needed a poo, when it dawned on me that I had shoved charcoal up my ass. The human in me found it all too hard to process. I took a moment to reflect, whilst I burst into tears when I then reminded myself; I have something out of it to be grateful for. I had experienced the feeling of being the source of all existence. Through humility, I felt like I was surrounded by light beings, to bear witness to Christ's consciousness. I felt comforted and supported and, whilst being laughed at by the others, I was amazed by what came next. The most soothing, most comfortable voice inside me gently said, "This is fate. 'You are meant to write about your life thus far, have courage. The prospects will far outweigh your discontent."

And so, I began this book. I first started writing it in the summer of 2020. I ended up giving up, after a couple of chapters. "There is fuck all about me," I thought. "I am not smart enough." But, looking at the bigger picture, I wasn't prepared to open up, terrified at the thought of putting myself under the spotlight. I worried what everyone would think of me, especially my family and anyone who knew me, should I decide to publish.

It wasn't until January 2021, when I met an author coach who also specialised in trauma, and could hold space for my story like my spiritual mentor, that I took the plunge and picked up my book again. From there, it took around seven months to complete.

If I'm honest with you, I felt like I had nothing to lose. What else was I going to do with my life? Carry on as a plasterer, miserable for the rest of my life? If you can recall, in the lesson for chapter one, I had already formed my biggest dream; to make a difference in the world, to be an inspiration.

So, I began by writing the outline for this book and reliving every traumatic experience I have lived to date (for the record, I recommend doing this with a professional who can hold you through it, too). It was somewhat of a desperation to figure myself out, noting everything down, from my earliest memory up until now. Over the course of writing this book, I have had to relive every moment, over and over again. I have been scared to my wits' end, discussing my addictions, sharing what I got up to, in and out of my family home, and in particular, this last chapter.

Sometimes, I would ask myself, why am I doing this to myself? Why would I even bring this kind of attention to myself? I felt so vulnerable at times, being as transparent as I have been in this book, that I would have rather deleted it altogether.

Surprisingly, what happened at the start of 2020, with the UK lockdowns, gave me courage. I had already recognised that shadow work meant to take off the mask! And with the pandemic, I saw the shadows come out on a collective level. Everyone was wearing a mask and covering their identity, physically and metaphorically. Most of them were unaware that, even when they took off the cloth, they were still wearing one mask after another. Some were heavy, others were ego, most were a false sense of security. Throughout this book, you have seen me shed layers upon layers of my own masks, because I believe that encouraging vulnerability is real strength.

I've been encouraged, by sharing my story, to believe the most important trait and virtue we can have of all is bravery.

We're all born to die. That is the truth, is it not? Yet, at the height of the pandemic, we were made to feel as though we should be frightened of death. I, for one, recognised, in relation to my own self, that I was hardly living at all, but merely existing, to begin with. I wondered, how many like myself can relate to that? How many are hiding behind the illusion of responsibility, detached from reality, from their own selves? Most of us hardly ever bring our own selves to centre stage or bring our own shadows to light.

Most of us crave the attention of others, getting to know them, wanting to be understood. This is a false sense of security, the feeling of belonging. In truth, though we rarely do it, true security is giving our own selves the connection we crave from others. Understanding ourselves.

From your fingerprint to your life experiences, there will never be another like you. You are unique and should never compare yourself with another. I came to find that out the hard way. Just look at this last chapter, believing that I had to sacrifice myself for the good of everyone else.

Although, as I write these words, I really do feel as though I am sacrificing my own ego, my last mask. It's left me feeling exposed and vulnerable at the hands of the world, but it is my hope it inspires another human being to be brave. If I can change even one person's life, I have made a difference.

I wonder if many of us genuinely believe in something far greater than ourselves. If not, then it's no wonder we have very little belief in one another. Faith is the opposite of fear. It is that understanding that helped me recognise and reframe my shame and guilt. They were an illusion, and a matter of where I decided to invest my energy. As I said in one of the earlier chapters, where you place your attention is where your energy goes.

Your shadow work is to strip off the masks you present to the world. Feel into this process, have a little tidy up, call it a day, wake up in the morning, and make your bed. Go again. In most of my chapters, I have left you lessons to help you do exactly that. You can either choose to become a little bit more vulnerable, a little bit braver, and strip off each mask as you work through the lessons, or you can choose to carry on playing the same old story that defines and shapes your life and character.

If I can find the courage to lay it all bare, so can you! If I can face up to my 'shame', so can you.

You might recall, at one point, I mentioned in one of the chapters that, if I could turn back the hands of time, I wouldn't change a thing. Now, I'll ask you the same...would you? There is no right or wrong answer here, so long as you're transparent with yourself. Do what I have done. Take your experiences; whether good or bad, you wouldn't have the knowledge you have now, and use them as a map to understand yourself. To know where you want to go. To navigate away from making the same mistakes. To learn what works for you and what doesn't.

Remember, your experiences don't define you. You are the one defining your life. You can choose to define it in healthier ways and be grateful for the lessons. Use me as an example. I transmuted it all with welcoming arms, in the hope it would help another, and I helped myself in the process.

It's now your turn to transform whatever negative thoughts, beliefs or experiences you might have and make them work for you. Make them positive.

EPILOGUE: SHOWTIME

Before that magic mushroom ceremony, when I was still in the beginning stages of my self-love journey, I was really depressed. I couldn't stand my life, if I was being honest. I was back at my parents', I didn't have a pot to piss in, was still managing my heartbreak, and I no longer enjoyed my job.

If it wasn't for psychedelics, I can't imagine what I might have ended up like. Where would I have been now? Where would I have been in my head? In my heart? DMT came into my life and connected me with my soul. Before then, well. You have read my story. If not for the realisation, the epiphany, the understanding of what faith means ... this story would have never been shared.

I thank you for going down this healing journey with me, and witnessing my own growth. I pray you are inspired, and now know wholeheartedly that the most important relationship there will ever be, is the one with your own self!

No one ever wakes up in the morning and says, "Today I am going to have a horrible day, how can I make today the worst day ever?" The trouble is, no one wakes up in the morning and gives themselves a kiss on the hand and says, "Have the best day ever, you absolute legend," either.

It's so important to have a heart to heart with yourself. It's so important to open up to others. It's so important to express your truth. Then, why is it that most of us don't? I believe it's because we have forgotten that, to do so, is in the spirit to offer comfort, to offer love, and to offer support to one another. Those fundamentals never cease to be just because we grow and mature! I believe we never cease to be children, and that we ought to remain young at heart.

I believe that life is about creating the best version of yourself, packaging that up, and giving it away. You have to be willing to completely expose who you are to the world, to be transparent. That's how you allow yourself the freedom to receive what you are worthy of, and live life at the top of your game.

If you want to see a change, well then, be the change!

You have to be awaiting your own arrival. You have to want to let go of the old ways and embrace the new you. You have to want to transition into a new way of being. Letting go of your past, in order to ascend, is your biggest friend. You have got to want love, and you have to want truth, not just for yourself, but for everyone else as well.

That comes at the cost of letting go of the narrative

you've been telling to date, and rewriting the script.

The toughest person to forgive is often oneself. It takes a lot of guts to accept who you really are and where you're currently at. That you made the choices that got you here. But you don't just forgive yourself when you're feeling lenient. You forgive yourself, and you rise up, regardless.

It's a process, building trust, building respect, building more love, setting the foundations for what your legacy will be, the day you cease to be of this body. And take it from me, just because you begin your healing journey, it doesn't mean things just as quickly get "fixed". But they *do* start to improve. Little by little, day by day.

Do you remember the legend of the Dark King? His eyes were as black as night and his soul was plagued by chaos, for his shadows would never leave him. He finally remembered that he was not The Dark King, but A Knight of the Light. That was who he was born to be.

And that is who *you* are. Your job is to awaken, to stop chasing the illusion in front of you, and to answer the call of who you really are.

That is the lockdown on self-love.

AUTHOR'S NOTE

I would like to, first of all, say thank fuck this has now come to an end, excuse my language. As you might have imagined, this whole book-writing process has been very emotional and, at the best of times, intense. Sitting with my inner turmoil, confronting all that I've repressed over the years, has not been easy, looking into the darkest depths of my soul. Deciding to write sure came with its challenges, many times feeling like wanting to give up altogether. I've lost count of the number of times I screamed in my head, "What are you even doing? Don't go there! How will others view you?" With the intention to then publish, feeling like the "damage" would then be irreversible. That I'd be a laughing stock, shamed and judged. All I can say is the following: I recognised strength and courage I never knew I had.

Strength and courage that lie within us all.

We can either look fear in the eyes and say, "Let's go," or we can remain in our cave and starve. Can you imagine us as a species, in our primitive days as cavemen? The terrain filled with dinosaurs, sabretooths, and predators alike? This analogy beautifully ties in with this whole book-writing process. If man, in the first instance, didn't have the courage to grab his spear and go hunt, once their resources had run low, his family wouldn't have survived.

So, how did I survive through this? If I'm honest with you, I felt like I had a moral obligation to do so. I felt like I had found my purpose and recognised what I was giving my life to. What else was I going to do? Spend the rest of my life, living and working as a plasterer? Miserable, most likely...

Truth be told, I also felt called to use all my suffering to my advantage. I felt like, whatever dirty secrets I had, that others might be gossiping about, I might as well call myself out on them. I could put them to use instead, make something positive happen. From there, a passion grew for wanting to help others who might also be suffering in silence, like I was myself.

What were the chances, if I hadn't; might I have otherwise eventually overdosed? It's happened to others who had habits as bad as mine. My insecurities were unbearable to live with, as well; that is no way to live...

Like I said, while this was the positive alternative, it was by no means easy.

I started in early 2020, as soon as the first lockdown happened. I had a rough idea of what the chapters would look like, and I proceeded to write chapter one, now known as the introduction of this book. I ended up closing the laptop, when I realised I would have to talk about my childhood, and what would then unfold to writing about the rest of my life. I hadn't relived the book, until meeting Ali Chambers, my mentor throughout this process, several months later.

There were a couple of chapters that were particularly difficult. It took a lot to keep pushing through from chapter three. But by chapter nine and ten, I couldn't quite believe how I was articulating myself. I wanted to soften the whole narrative, I wanted to make it more "socially acceptable" & to protect myself. I took a moment to refocus on why I was writing this book, which was to speak my truth, advocate transparency and that vulnerability is a true testament to strength. With that in mind, I stayed focused & was really honest. I gave my true account and felt proud of myself for being so brave.

There were many other chapters I found hard to confront and relive. At this point, I was still healing from heartbreak and rebuilding my life. Then, in late 2021, chapter seventeen happened, and God knows, that was the most difficult chapter of them all. If any of the chapters warranted me giving up on my dream, it was that one. It was a huge test, to see how far I was willing to go. I was scared out of my wits, although I then realised something beautiful from it; this book wouldn't have been a powerful read, without that ending.

I still don't know where I got the strength to push through and make this whole book come alive. The only thing I can say is that I believed in something far greater than myself and decided to go full steam ahead, either way. I didn't want to, one day, be on my death bed, aware of my cowardice.

So, here I am, having decided to give myself the biggest opportunity I've had to date. To own who I am. This is such a beautiful gift one can offer him/herself.

I have come to understand that the most important relationship there will ever be and is, is the one with yourself. You have the responsibility to take care of yourself, understand how you are treating yourself and what you are giving your life, too.

I had to get really honest with myself – for example, what were my beliefs about who I was? What was my relationship with life? With money, for example? And all of life's many gifts. What were the views that held me back from living to my full potential? What was my attitude? Who was it that I decided, each new day, to be? Because, when you think about it, who you are being is everything that shapes your world and interactions within it.

You have to be really honest with yourself. So, my final exercise to give you, is the following. Ask yourself, what is going wrong? What do I know I am doing wrong, that I could fix, if only I would fix it? That is also why I chose to call the subtitle for this book; how to make suffering work for you.

The truth might be scary, and it sure scared me. The truth is what sets us all free, however, and our creative reservoir is what then creates our future. By being really honest about all the things we can change, we can begin to address them, one by one, and find resolution. We owe it to ourselves; we owe it to one another. Furthermore, being in denial won't help. And it won't set the standard for our children and future generations, either. We must want for them what we have needed for ourselves, all this time.

So, where am I now on my journey & what answers did I find in the exercise that I shared with you?

I had to get honest about my addictions. I didn't smoke weed often, but always had this sense of awareness that it wasn't helping. Sometimes, it heightened my insecurities and, other times, it made me feel like a bit of a doughnut. I knew, deep down, I ought to quit, be focused, and I would improve, as an individual.

Truth be told, I also ended up back on steroids, at one point. But I made a plan to get off them and committed to doing 50 push ups every morning, while I was waiting for the kettle to boil.

The cocaine habit, I've managed to keep at bay. When temptation once in a while creep ups, I recommit back to my lessons. Staying away from these substances has taught me discipline, and as someone once told me, discipline is the highest form of self-love.

From here, I will continue to better myself and will eventually look to volunteer at mental health institutes and be of better service to others. I want to surround myself with others, who practice and promote abstinence in the face of pornographic and sexual addictions, as well.

If you come to think of it, we were all born from our mothers, we're a gift to the world and it is a privilege to just be of existence. This human life is precious. What I have learned through this, is that sex is sacred, and it ought to be treated as such.

It's of concern to think that, for most of my life, I used drugs. But, when you think about it, it's a shame that is "socially acceptable" to go to the shops and buy as many packets of fags as you like and as much alcohol as you can drink, to drown your sorrows and escape from your responsibilities. Or visit the doctor to get a prescription and, again, numb ourselves with chemicals, for whatever reason, which is acceptable but doesn't resolve the issues.

My drug addiction started with cigarettes, caving to peer pressure and wanting to fit in. From there, it became marijuana. They say that marijuana is the gateway drug, but I don't believe that's true. I think the trauma we experience, that makes us want to be numb in the first place, is the true gateway.

The psychedelics or "plant medicine" might also alarm some readers. You might think I've only gone from one drug to another and that I'm only using plant medicine to escape my own reality. Let me assure you, this is not the case. By no means.

The difference here is that this isn't something taken likely and something you could recreationally do. It is something that is treated with respect, something I like to call the Holy Grail; a compound that has been suppressed from humankind, that connects you with your soul and gives you defining proof there is more to life than we are led to believe. It takes a great deal of courage to use the healing properties of plant medicine and discover the insights into the biggest questions found in these altered states of consciousness. I came to find myself, but I by no means promote it.

It's for each individual's discretion and there is enough research online for you to look into it for yourself, if you wish to know if it's right for you.

For myself, I'm thankful it introduced a new element of spirituality to me. It initiated me into my personal development journey, and I'm so thankful for meditation and the many benefits of the journey I'm on.

So, what am I looking forward to, having completed this book?

I look forward to integrating the many lessons I've shared with you in this book and putting them into practice. I look forward to diving deeper into the mystical arts and going on retreats of all sorts, to meet other like-minded people.

I now have a new vision, to speak on stage about my passions, to be of service and inspire. I'm choosing to be that guy others can confide in, having led by example, to show that sharing your truth is an honourable trait to have. It works in your favour and can give others the safety to express their own truth, too.

Because, people can only meet you where they meet themselves.

By the way, you might wonder what happened to my curiosity around my prostate. Truthfully, I have yet to experience what I wanted to, all this time. I think that is why I spiralled out of control more, with the drugs in the first place; it formed into a unhealthy obsession, a fantasy. But since bettering myself, I've shut that door behind me. It's nice to also acknowledge that I have made peace with it and no longer feel ashamed about it. Who knows, maybe one day I'll have the safety of a relationship with that special lady, and we can experiment with our bodies, in healthier ways. Until then, I'll practice abstinence, as best I can.

It gave me a great deal of comfort to discover what is natural in my body, and all the other many organs we have; their functions, how the human mind, too, works and all its mysticism. For all the times we are led to believe we are abnormal for our wants, desires, and addictions, that bring about shame, and more trauma, I hope this book has helped you make peace with them all, as well - as it has for me.

Remember, get really honest with yourself. Cut out all the excuses. Identify the challenges you face, create a plan. Implement the lessons you learn; whatever happened, or happens, at the very least, don't let them be in vain. Choose better for yourself. And last but not least, allow the best to unfold.

I'll be seeing you in my next book, with a totally different story from the one you've read here.

Excited about the future ahead...

Antonio de Sousa

ACKNOWLEDGEMENTS

There are so many names I would like to give thanks to for their help in my life and in this book-writing process. Firstly, my parents for having invited me to their loving home and being so supportive. Without you both, none of this would have been possible. The safety you provided is what allowed me to flourish and grow.

I also want to thank Veena Raynes and Krisztina Konya. I don't know how I would have coped without you. Your kindness and belief in me has left me speechless on many accounts. You have helped in more ways than you know. If not for you two, I may have quit this project, like I was close to doing, so many times.

Thank you to Ali Chambers, my mentor throughout this writing process.

And to so many others I would like to thank, but I don't want to miss anyone out accidentally, so I will just say; you know who you are. Thank you.

ABOUT THE AUTHOR

Antonio De Sousa, formerly a plasterer by trade, gives his true account of what it is like to be a man who once hated himself. He acknowledges life hasn't been easy. With codependency and a predisposition for drugs, and a break up that led him to question his life, along with a victim mentality, Antonio has embarked on improving the fragile relationship he had with himself, in his debut book; The Lockdown on Self-Love.

Antonio promotes transparency and advocates that vulnerability is real strength, in his work. He gives voice to sensitive subjects that many men have suffered with. He loves to share these principles with others, with a dose of personal development and spirituality, to inspire others to realise that the most important relationship there will ever be and is, is the one you have with yourself.

He is also a proud father of two young children.

To learn more about Antonio De Sousa visit:

www.U-Volve.co.uk

Thank you for reading! If you enjoyed this book and would like to share your thoughts please feel free to leave a review on Amazon or a similar site. Book reviews help spread the word and help readers find great books.

Printed in Great Britain
by Amazon

18410225R00171